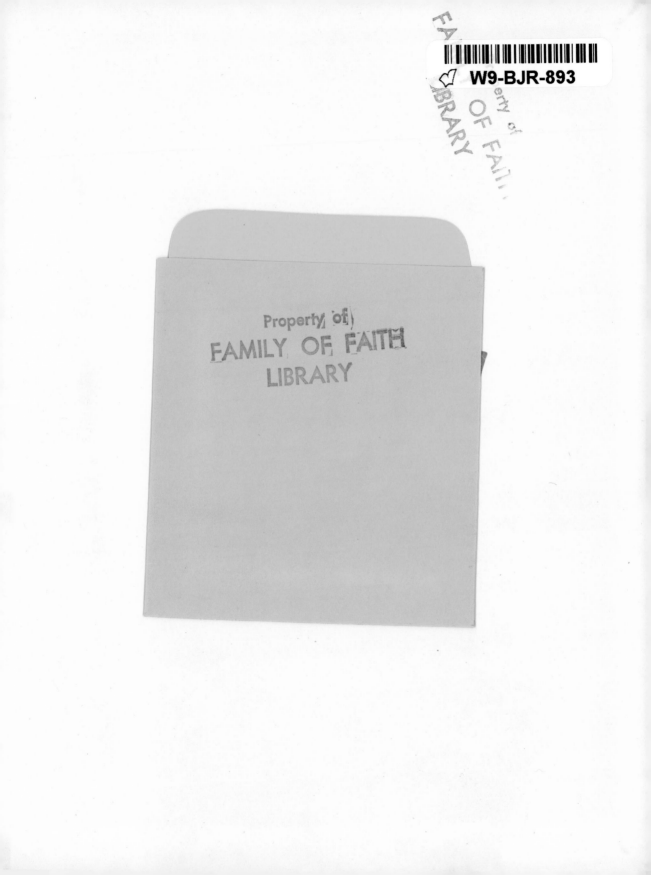

PRACTICAL WRITING IN BUSINESS AND INDUSTRY

PRACTICAL WRITING IN BUSINESS AND INDUSTRY

PAUL M. ZALL

California State University, Los Angeles

LEONARD N. FRANCO

Pasadena City College

DUXBURY PRESS   North Scituate, Massachusetts

Library of Congress Cataloging in Publication Data

Franco, Leonard N.
  Practical writing in business and industry.
  Includes index.
  1. Commercial correspondence. 2. Business report writing. 3. English language—Business English. I. Zall, Paul M., joint author. II. Title.
HF5721.F73   651.7'4   77-12042
ISBN 0-87872-141-X

Duxbury Press
A Division of Wadsworth Publishing Company, Inc.

Practical Writing in Business and Industry was edited and prepared for composition by Jane Lovinger. Cover design was by Garrow Throop.

L.C. Cat. Card No.: 77-12042
ISBN 0-87872-141-X
Printed in the United States of America
  2 3 4 5 6 7 8 9 — 82 81 80 79

CONTENTS

PREFACE

    This is a book about writing for people not trained as writers, but who find themselves having to write as a part of their professional lives. The book was developed many years ago, before we became professors, when we worked together in the aerospace industry during the hectic race to put a man on the moon. We were astonished to see how many of our professional colleagues, all experts in their fields, dreaded the act of writing even a simple memorandum. They simply misunderstood what was expected of them. No one expected them to write as brilliantly as Ernest Hemingway or as easily as their favorite sports writer. Yet no one told them otherwise, and so, in their ignorance, they labored mightily to bring forth a mountain of bad writing. Moved by the recollection of those bad times, we have tried to bring about a new awareness of just what is expected from nonprofessional writers engaged in practical writing.

    In this book we have tried to give a sense of what it is like to write in a business-industrial environment, with one eye on budgets and the other on schedules, your mind on the problem at hand, and your emotions tied up in the act of writing. For this purpose we developed a fictional firm, Bellco. Bellco is a large, diversified corporation engaged in business, engineering, and manufacturing — a company large enough to provide a variety of problems common in firms of any size. The practices and procedures, as well as the problems, which were developed for Bellco over the past twenty years, form the substance of this book. Any similarity to reality is intentional.

    In the Introduction to Part One we discuss the difference between the practical writing required by Bellco and the kind of writing more familiar in advertising and journalism. But, that is the limit of theorizing. Thereafter, the book proceeds step-by-step through problems in practical writing, from planning a résumé for Bellco's employment office to composing a full-scale proposal seeking government business. The unique emphasis given to preparing résumés and proposals reflects the two-fold emphasis of the whole book — to provide practical information and to develop basic principles of good writing practice. Knowing how to prepare a résumé to meet different requirements is basic to knowing how to write letters or reports with different requirements. Writing form and style are adjusted to the document's function and the reader's needs. Subsequent chapters in the first part of the book develop the principles established in the first chapter and lead to their large-scale application in the final chapter on proposals.

Because we recognize that writing is a science as well as an art, the second part of the book provides a ready-reference guide to solving specific problems in grammar and style, even proofreading. An appendix offers sample documents readily adaptable to a variety of needs, but with the caution that each writing assignment has its own special set of requirements and constraints.

The book is designed as a self-teaching text for individual readers as well as for use in classrooms or seminars. College classes will find value in following the chapters in sequence, moving from simple to more complex problems. Industrial training programs or professional seminars might find it more valuable to focus on certain problem areas. In either case, the many exercises are intentionally open-ended to provide a basis for discussion and to reemphasize that seldom is there an arbitrary, clear-cut formula for solving problems involving people. Each problem must be tackled on its own terms with due regard for local issues. At the same time, such problems can only profit from collective common sense and a feeling for the right thing to do in a given circumstance.

Finally, the book is designed for long-range use as a desk-reference text throughout a professional career. We have avoided fads in favor of proven principles that will long endure.

With respect to our own stylistic practices, we gratefully acknowledge that they have benefited immeasurably from the expert editing of Jane G. Lovinger, Betty Patterson, and Edward L. Francis. May all writers be so fortunate in their editors! For invaluable suggestions and support through the early going, we are also indebted to Marie Pibel, Nancy Craven, and Lyle Waters.

L.N.F.
P.M.Z.

PART ONE -- WHAT YOU WILL BE WRITING

THIS BOOK IS ABOUT practical writing. Our aim is to provide quick aid for the more common problems faced every day by people who are not trained writers but find themselves having to write as part of their work. Our focus is on practical writing — as opposed to the kind of writing you read on the sports pages, in a novel, or in advertising.

PRACTICAL WRITING IS PROBLEM SOLVING

Most of the everyday writing in business, industry, or government agencies consists of answering questions, providing quick information, or calling attention to some need or condition that needs fixing.

Very seldom is the nonprofessional writer called upon to write the kind of elaborate formal report taught in school or featured in most textbooks (including this one). Most writing is done in brief memorandums ("memos"), for the purpose of supplying quick information or making a record of activities. Frequently this involves merely filling in blanks on printed forms. But as persons move upward on the occupational ladder, they find themselves having to write more and more independently, and more and more different kinds of documents.

The Aim of Practical Writing Is to Inform

Its aim is to teach rather than preach, tell rather than sell. Its primary goal is to help readers arrive at a thoughtful decision based on all available pertinent facts.

Some practical writing commonly includes recommendations about what the reader should think, do, or expect to happen. This comes close to selling instead of telling. The difference is the relative balance between fact and opinion. In Figure I–1, the memo begins with a statement of fact. The second paragraph subtly slips away from straight reporting with the word "cradles" ("locks" or "holds" would have described a more important function of the cap, without the emotional overtones). The third paragraph begins with straight fact, then brings in opinion with "quicker . . . easier . . . safer"; it concludes with nothing but opinion.

Life in the final quarter of the twentieth century is conditioned by advertising slogans that blur the distinction between fact and opinion. One of the most successful advertising writers, Shirley Polykoff, is famous for these slogans — not one of which makes a statement of fact: "Does she . . . or doesn't she? Only her hairdresser knows for sure." "If I have but one life, let me live it as a blonde." "Is it true blondes have more fun?" Ironically, Ms. Polykoff also wrote these famous slogans: "Every woman should be a redhead at least once in her life." "You can be a rich brunette (the kind men marry)." Even though her statements are not factual and do compete with one another, they are good examples of

TO: Hal Garrison, Manager of Marketing

FROM: Eleanor Mason, Marketing

SUBJECT: New Product Development - Safety Pin

You will be pleased to know that we have developed the Safety Pin, a fastening device designed to be a low-cost replacement for buttons, zippers, and straight pins.

The Safety Pin is a thin, durable, lightweight metal clasp. One end is pointed to pierce cloth material. The other end is shaped as a safety cap that cradles the pointed end when the pin is closed.

Models come in sizes from 1 cm to 6 cm for various thicknesses of cottons, woolens, and synthetic cloth. Prices have not yet been set but the Safety Pin should retail at only slightly higher than the straight pin, with far greater safety. Quicker to use than needle-and-thread, easier than buttons, and safer than zippers, the Safety Pin promises to revolutionize fastening.

Figure 1-1
A Memo that Sells Instead of Informing.

her kind of writing, writing that makes an emotional appeal. They sold a fortune in hair colors. But they would be out of place in our kind of writing.

The easiest way to see the distinction is in this chart; it shows attributes of advertising writing in one row and of practical writing in the other. When you consider that people find it easier to "think" emotionally, you can understand why they would find advertising more exciting than practical writing. But, at the same time, consider what would happen if decisions in business, industry, and government were

	Goal	Deals With	Approach	Information	Appeal
Advertising	emotion	opinion	indirect	distorted	emotional
Practical Writing	decision	fact	direct	accurate	logical

based on emotion rather than thoughtful, reasonable choices which practical writing is designed to encourage.

PRACTICAL WRITING IS SELLING, BUT ONLY OF YOURSELF

You are selling yourself as someone who knows what he's talking about. And you want your readers to believe that what you say is so. Therefore you present your information as expertly and convincingly as you can.

An old saying among lawyers goes: "If you have the facts, argue from the facts. If you have the law, argue from the law. If you have neither the facts nor the law, make a lot of noise." But as a writer you do not have those options. Practical writing has to stick to the facts. Its conclusions and recommendations must derive from the information it provides; and that information must be provided impartially, logically, and clearly. Failures must be reported along with successes. Negative results may prove just as valuable as positive results. Reporting a mistake may prevent its happening again. Be scrupulously honest!

PRACTICAL WRITING SATISFIES THE EXPECTATIONS OF ITS READERS

A reader will expect to be informed, not entertained or subjected to a hard sell. He looks for information that is complete for the purpose at hand, accurate, and not distorted.

Practical writing follows familiar patterns. Just as you know where to find certain features in your newspaper, so a reader of practical writing expects to find certain kinds of information in certain places, or arranged in familiar "formats." Likewise, he will expect the writing to follow a procedure familiar to you from a good lecture: SUMMARIZING the most important point at the beginning, CLARIFYING that point with examples of facts and figures, and EMPHASIZING what those facts and figures show.

We expect the professional writer to turn out a highly polished product in short order. But the sometime writer who does not have the professional's experience should not expect to equal the professional's achievement or ease. Take heart — *the more you write, the easier it is to write.*

APPLYING FOR A JOB 👉
1

THE RÉSUMÉ

S o you want to get a job. Good! Applying for a job with any company is going to be a three-step process: preparing a file on yourself, putting together a résumé, and writing a letter of application. You have every reason to expect success if you present your credentials with the proper emphasis, style, and interest.

Most companies are eager to employ college-trained personnel in a wide variety of positions. The one common determinant of all these positions is that they are likely to require communications skills. In many companies, communications is the most important problem — both within the company and in relationships with suppliers and customers.

You can assume that your résumé and letter of application will be given careful and prompt consideration in most of the companies to which you will apply. If a match-up occurs between your background and education and an available job, then you stand a good chance of getting the job. But in addition, even if your qualifications are not suitable for an open position, your communications skills might land you a job with a company that recognizes and needs individuals with exceptional skills to help the staff improve its memorandums, letters, reports, and proposals. In any case, no effort you make toward improving your communications skills is ever wasted effort.

GATHERING DATA ON POSSIBLE EMPLOYERS

When you apply for a job you can be sure that you will be scrutinized by the company. Its representatives will check on your references, delve into your background, perhaps even talk to relatives and friends. Why should it be all one way? It shouldn't. You can survey them too. You should be devising questions and seeking answers to them so that you can better assess the company as your potential employer.

A job is a job is a job, to paraphrase Gertrude Stein. But should it be only that? You don't want to work for a company for a few months, only to find out that you're unhappy and frustrated. Avoid this situation by doing some careful research and planning prior to submitting a formal résumé or application.

If you're interested in working for a company in a certain industry, find out about both the company and the industry. Each company you apply to is different. There are several things you'll want to know about every firm you consider: What kind of a company is it? What does it do? What industry is it a part of? What are its products or services? Almost every company distributes a lot of free literature on itself and its products. One very informative publication is the annual report, which provides information to investors; it usually includes such information as a report to shareholders, a review of operations, a review of products and services, a description of the organization and management structure, and a financial review. The annual report often contains tables and graphs on the company's performance over the last five or six years and projections of the company's potential for additional growth.

Try the Library

Many companies — local, national, international — are listed in a variety of publications available in the reference sections of most town libraries. These publications will give you an overview of most industries in the country and a breakdown of the companies within the industry.

Start with *The Occupational Outlook Handbook* published by the U.S. Department of Labor Statistics. This document provides information on industry trends and on companies within various industries and businesses. It includes sections on the outlook for industries: agriculture, mining and petroleum, construction, manufacturing, transportation, communications, public utilities, wholesale and retail trade, finance, insurance, real estate, government, and services. It also describes numerous occupations in sales, scientific and technical work, office work, and the social sciences. The job description includes information on job responsibility, job outlook, earnings, training required, and places of employment.

Publications such as the *Industry Surveys* published by Standard and Poor, Moody's *Manuals*, the *College Placement Annual*, and the Dun and Bradstreet *Million Dollar Directory* will also help. There are more, many more. The reference librarian will be glad to assist you.

Don't neglect the yellow pages of local phone books. They can provide a list of local companies in your field of interest. Trade publications, too, provide useful information within the field and help you assess "your company's" standing. Of course general business publications should not be ignored; for example, *Fortune, Business Week, Barrons*, the *Wall Street Journal*. These publications provide current business information on industries, companies, and business trends and cycles. For instance, the *Wall Street Journal* is a daily publication which provides stock and bond market reports, articles on various industry activities, and insights into potential problem areas.

Make Lists

Write everything down: names of companies, addresses, names of executives, products, sales, profits, and so on. Either duplicate book pages or take copious notes because it's very frustrating to have to go back time and time again to look up the same material. Efficient use of job-hunting time is often the key to finding the right position. A day or two in the local library should provide you with enough information to write as many application letters as you want. For ideas in making lists more effective, see the Troubleshooter's Guide, paragraphs 8.6 to 8.9.

WHO ARE YOU?
YOUR CREDITS AND DEBITS

You have surveyed the field; now survey yourself. Prepare a list of items from your background and experience. This will be a list that only you will see or use. From it you will select the information that will constitute your résumé, so make it complete. You will want to divide your list into categories similar to those which appear on most résumés — such as education, work experience, personal factors, and references. You will get the information you need if you ask yourself questions about yourself.

Education

You might begin by listing in reverse chronological order (starting with the most recent and working backward) the schools you attended, addresses, dates, degrees, credentials or certificates earned, courses taken, honors, and scholarships. In which subjects did you get the best grades? In which subjects did you do poorly? Why? What specialty courses have you taken — data processing, computer programming, typing, stenography, business machines, communications? List everything that pertains to your education; don't be concerned too much with emphasis or order, that will come later. Concentrate now on completeness. Did you do a senior project? Did you perform a special study? Write them down and include any pertinent facts.

After you have completed your listing of all elements pertaining to your education, take out a separate paper and divide it down the center. On one side write the heading *Credits*, on the other side, *Debits*. Now under credits write your strengths — i.e., majors, minors, honors, awards, subjects you liked, subjects you did well in. Under debits write your weak areas: majors changed because the work was too difficult or not interesting, subjects you did poorly in or didn't like, communications problems with teachers, fellow students, or others. Is there anything you can do to minimize the debits? Sometimes not. (You may not be interested in journalism and those two years as a journalism major showed you that. However, on the credit side, you should list the skills you developed while in the program.) See the sample credit/debit page, which is Table 1-1.

Education

Credits	Debits
Major: Business Administration Expect to graduate in June.	
Best Areas: Communications Marketing	*Weak Areas:* Math Accounting
Communications: Excelled in the following courses:	*Math:* Bus. Math C
Business English A Business Communications A Report Writing A Speech B Was selected to write model sales letter for Business Department publication. Wrote two proposals and one report; received A on all three.	Also took Beginning Calculus and dropped at 3 weeks. Just not my cup of tea. Don't like numbers or working with them. Did learn to use a calculator, though.
Marketing: Did well in following:	*Accounting:* Found it boring—Got a C in
Sales A Merchandising A General Marketing B Particularly liked simulated selling situations. Confident and convincing. Chosen by Business Department to attend (as student representative) Sales Convention in L.A.	the first semester; really didn't deserve it. Same problems I had w/Business Math.
Other: Did well in Business Law (B) and Introduction to Business (A).	*Other:* Business Psychology. I thought I'd do well, but I didn't. Lucky to get a C. Could have been the way the subject was taught. Would have liked more case histories.

Table 1-1
*A Sample
Credit/Debit Page
Concerning
Education*

Experience

Even if you have only worked at part-time positions while attending school, you should list all the jobs you have had. Designate that they were part time and note what you did and for how long. For all jobs, you should carefully list (again reverse chronological order helps) any job titles, duties, dates, supervisors' names and titles, names of other key personnel you may want to use as references.

Ask yourself questions about your work experience: What did you do well? What did you enjoy doing? And what did you do least well? What did you dislike doing? Now, take another paper and divide it down the center. Head one side *Credits* and the other *Debits.* Chances are if you disliked selling over the telephone, you probably did poorly at it, so that experience goes down as a debit; you would want to avoid a future position that emphasized telephone sales.

Did you gain any special knowledge on any of your previous jobs, or any special skills? List them. How well did you get along with people on the job? How well did you communicate your ideas in writing or orally? Would you consider your communications skills a credit or a debit? If a debit, and this goes for any item on that side of the center line, what can you do about it? Consider whether you should go back to school, take an evening class, enroll in a correspondence course, or start on a self-help program on your own.

Your dossier on your education and experience should contain a list of all the factual data on your school and job history and additional pages on your strengths and weaknesses separated into credits and debits. Careful review of these may reveal some behavior pattern to you. For instance, if you didn't like and did poorly in written communications in college, you would certainly want to think carefully before accepting a job in which you were expected to write memos and letters. Chances are you would do poorly on the job, too. You would want to avoid jobs which stress written communications — unless you are willing to take some improvement programs or courses to try to move that debit over to the credit side of the line. These are options you have. The decision is really up to you and no one else. It is not necessary for you to try to eliminate all the debits, but common sense says you should know of their existence in order to plan wisely.

You now have the two basic elements to prepare a strong résumé, but, before you do, you would do well to make at least two more lists: one of personal factors and one of references.

Personal Factors

These include your name, address, date of birth, marital status, height, weight, general physical condition, hobbies, interests, organizations, publications, and languages. Some of these elements, particularly languages and publications, could be included in your lists of education and experience, but in this instance let's consider them here.

You can design a credit/debit page here, too. You would want to examine your personality (and try to be as objective as possible) and list traits. Do you like people? Are you easy to get along with? Do you cope well under stress? If you were offered a job writing proposals for new business, you would have to work around-the-clock for periods of time to meet certain deadlines. Could you accept this requirement, or is your schedule so structured that you couldn't possibly accommodate such a drastic change? It helps to know these things about yourself before you go job seeking.

Try to imagine how the credits of your personality will match up with general types of job requirements. Try, also, to think of jobs in which personality debits will not be significant. For example, suppose that you are gregarious and that you are looking into jobs in marketing: that combination is a good match-up. But what if you were interested in marketing but found it difficult to meet new people: you might really struggle in a marketing job, and not experience either success or pleasure. If, however, you do not enjoy meeting new people and your greatest job aspiration is to conduct independent research, the personality debit proves to be of little consequence. A personality debit is not going to be magically transformed into a credit just by job choice (at least not in most cases), but it can be effectively neutralized.

References

List all the people you know that you feel would provide a strong reference for you. Next to their names include addresses, home and work telephone numbers, job titles, relationship to you, dates to show how long you've known them, and personal comments on your relationship with them; include any problems in communications, personality compatibility, job conflicts. Be sure to comment on the personality of your reference. Was he well liked, not liked, did he perform his job well? After doing this for each potential reference, you may find a few that you'd like to take off the list. Better to do it now than to find out later, after you've submitted the name, that your reference responded with only a lukewarm recommendation.

If you know certain habits or traits that the proposed reference exhibits, put them down. For instance, someone you know to be a habitual procrastinator, especially when it comes to writing letters, may never respond to an inquiry about you. If you want to use him as a reference, you might want to call him from time to time to see if he's been contacted. In any event, you'll have alerted yourself to a potential problem and can devise a counterstrategy.

KEEPING YOUR FILES ACTIVE

You now are well on your way to having a file on yourself and a file on your job possibilities. Put them in separate folders but keep them handy, and near each other. You have gone through the process of "individual brainstorming." As you think of items you may have missed or neglected, add them. This is not a one-time-only proposition, not a dead file. It is dynamic and it represents you in words, so treat it that way. When you finish a course in business psychology, for instance, add it to the file. Check to see if it removes a debit and adds a credit.

ANALYZING THE DATA ON YOURSELF – USING A MATRIX

You have a job waiting for you somewhere. What you need to do now is take that file you've prepared, select the data you want to present, organize it for emphasis, prepare an outline, and develop your résumé. Your résumé may be the single most influential element in the presentation of yourself as candidate for a job opening.

A matrix, which is a device in which data can be displayed graphically in rows and columns, can help you stress the most useful factors in your résumé. If you know the requirements of the position for which you are applying and you know your strengths (from your credit list), you can prepare a job matrix on yourself. Along the abscissa (horizontally across the top of the grid), list all the job requirements you know about. Along the ordinate (vertically down the left-hand side of the grid), list all your strengths pertinent to the position. Check those boxes in which your strength matches a requirement.

You are attempting to find specific experiences from your background which fulfill expected requirements. (Of course, to be able to do this effectively, you need to know the job requirements.) The matrix allows you to keep the reader (your potential employer) in mind, and to write for him and to him.

The matrix in Figure 1-1 is an example of job requirements versus

Figure 1-1
A Sample Matrix Showing how an Applicant's Strengths Match up with the Requirements of a Job for Which He Is Applying.

▼

		JOB REQUIREMENTS -- REPORT WRITER			
		WRITING SHORT, INFORMAL REPORTS	WRITING LONG, FORMAL REPORTS	WRITING PROPOSALS	EDITING
BERNIE BASCOM'S STRENGTHS	ENGINEERING AIDE AT ATI FROM 1970-73	Wrote memos on design problems, coordination procedures, and new product developments	Helped staff prepare progress report on avionics system L-1040 for the Navy	Worked on L-1041 proposal (prepared related experience section)	----
	TECHNICIAN AT ELECTRO DEVICES 1968-1970	Wrote memos to supervisor on amplifier testing and tuning techniques	------	Helped prepare calibration section for advanced systems proposal to the Dept. of Interior	------
	REPORT WRITING AT LONG VIEW COLLEGE, IDAHO	Wrote memos on various subjects including technical, marketing, and finance	Wrote a formal report on nuclear power as a primary energy source	------	--------
	BUSINESS COMMUNICATIONS AT LONG VIEW COLLEGE	Wrote letters-- sales, credit, collection, persuasive	--------	Wrote a letter proposal on a new product.	Did some editing of other student papers

employee skills and education for the position of report writer at a medium-sized systems development company.

The job applicant of Figure 1-1, Bernie Bascom, has had experience as an engineering aide and technician, which does give him some background to stress in his résumé and letter of application for the job of report writer. He also took courses in college which complement his work experience. The matrix approach allows him to see these work and education experiences grouped on a single page and to relate them directly to the specific job requirements.

Let's look first at the ordinate (vertical) scale of the matrix. Mr. Bascom has filled this in with job titles, course titles, the places of the experiences, and the dates (in inverse chronological order). Along the abscissa he has written in the job requirements. In the appropriate blanks within the matrix, he has noted the specific function he performed which directly relates to the job requirement.

A glance at your own matrix will tell you which areas to stress in your résumé and letter of application. It can also help prepare you for the interview by pointing up those areas on which questions may be asked. It would be wise to examine carefully the blanks on the matrix and to prepare a response to a possible question regarding your background, or lack of it, in that area. If you have never worked on manuals, say so; however, you should read some manuals to understand the form, style, outline, and approach before you go to the interview. Then you can at least talk knowledgeably about them.

PRESENTING THE DATA ON YOURSELF

Many people think of the résumé as a data sheet or a fact sheet. It should be more than that: it should provide the reader, hopefully a prospective employer, with enough information on you to provoke an interview. That is the purpose of the résumé and the letter of application — to get you in for an interview. If you treat the résumé merely as a data sheet, you may as well just fill out the company's application blank (which you'll have to do anyway) and wait your turn.

As an individual, a separate personality, you have something to offer that no one else has. No single fact sheet or data sheet format can allow for that. You should *design your résumé around your strengths, your credits*. Make it fit you; don't try to fit someone else's format.

Many schools have résumé formats for students to use. You may want to use your school's format to list all the pertinent information from your file. But then look it over carefully — does it really suit you or is there a better arrangement of information? If you have any artistic or design background, now is the time to use it. Use space to heighten key pieces of information and to frame the résumé. You've probably been told to get everything on one page — but at what sacrifice? If you cram all the information you think should be presented onto one page, and it clutters and fills every section of the page, you've probably defeated your own purpose. The reader will feel like the tourist who walks into the Pitti Palace in Florence, Italy, and is overwhelmed by art masterpieces by Raphael, Donatello, DaVinci; they fill every inch of every room, including walls, ceilings, and cupboards. The viewer often retreats to the local café for a bit of espresso. So, too, your reader may withdraw — to the next uncluttered résumé.

It is true that there are specific elements of information the employer will want to see on the résumé. You will include items such as: job experience, education, personal characteristics, references, and perhaps a job objective. It is merely a question of how and where. The résumé is a sales tool, and the product you are selling is you.

There are two basic model formats of résumés and many, many variations. The two models are presented here because they are familiar and many personnel people relate well to them. But if they do not fit your needs, then go to a variation or an entirely new design. This need for flexibility pertains particularly to job seekers on the executive level, who should try to show innovation and imagination in their applications; after all, they will be expected to show those qualities on the job.

The Sequential Résumé

The sequential résumé presents everything in sequence, only it starts with the most recent and works backward through time. It is usually divided into the following parts:

Heading: Name, address, telephone number
Employment Objective: If you have a specific job in mind, cite it; if not,

you can probably discuss briefly the job area. For instance, you might list marketing, with emphasis on market research and planning.

Employment Experience: In this format, you start with your most recent job; provide dates of employment, name of employer and address, your job title, and a brief description of duties and responsibilities. You would also describe any unique or outstanding achievements on the job.

Education: Start with the latest schooling and again work in reverse chronological order. For example, graduate school: give dates attended, name the school, the degree obtained or any special certificates or credentials, your major, and identify courses directly related to your employment objective. Do the same for college and junior college. If you have completed high school but did not go on to college, do the same with your high school background. Be sure to include any scholarships or honors and your grade-point average if you have an outstanding one (3.0 or better on a 4-point scale).

Military Information: If you served in the military, you may want to include the experience, again by dates, in your employment experience.

Personal Data: The trend in personal data is not to include very much. You may include personal data which you feel will enhance your chance to win the job. This may include date of birth, designation of sex and of marital status, and a brief statement on the status of your health and your height and weight. Whether you include a picture of yourself is optional.

Supporting Data: If you have acquired special skills along the way but are not sure where they would be applicable, you may include a separate category to fit them: languages, business machines know-how, membership in professional organizations, publications, job-related hobbies. Chances are that if you arrange your résumé carefully, you can include these under employment experience or education.

References: If you are sending your résumé to a few selected companies, then it is reasonable to include references. Be sure that you have first notified the references that you are using their names. If you are sending your résumé to a random selection of companies, perhaps as many as 100, then do not include names of references on the résumé. Instead just say: references furnished upon request.

There is no reason why, in a sequential résumé, employment experience has to come before education. If you are a recent graduate and your education is your strength, then highlight it by putting it first, in the position of emphasis.

A sample sequential résumé is shown in Figure 1-2.

The Functional Résumé

If you were to combine your experience into functional categories (such as sales, management, communications, finance) and you included information on each, regardless of when or under whom the experience was gained, then you would be taking the functional approach to the résumé. An example of this approach is provided in Figure 1-3.

If you were in sales in 1972, 1973, and again in 1974–1976, you can combine all your experience under one heading, Sales. After all, it is still pertinent and valid, so why not eliminate the arbitrary barrier of time? Speak of the work as it should be spoken of — as a part of your background and development. Your continuing experience in sales is what should be important to your new employer. The names of the companies you worked for and the dates can be included at the end of the discussion.

When would you want to construct a functional résumé rather than a sequential one? Let's look at a situation in recent history for an illustration of the merits of the functional résumé.

In the late 1950s and again in the late 1960s and early 1970s, Southern California was beset with problems of unemployment in its major industry, aerospace. Employees who worked for companies such as Douglas, North American Rockwell, Hughes, and Lockheed found it difficult to find jobs in so-called commercial business or with commercial industries. This term, commercial, was used to designate businesses that did not deal exclusively, or primarily, with the government. Among these companies there was a stigma attached to ex-aerospace workers. They were, according to the prevailing stereotype, overpaid, used to luxury on the job, used to high overhead and general and administrative expense, and generally not profit oriented. Many very competent, efficient, and effective prospects were not hired because of this stigma.

The functional résumé can help to overcome the handicap of a stigma. Instead of presenting a company name (such as Lockheed or Boeing) to a new employer, who may be wary of the background (stereotype) this implies, the functional résumé lets him read about the strengths of the individual. The potential employer is able to see how the individual

Mary Jane Johnson

2500 Foothill Street

Pasadena, California 91001

453-6471

EMPLOYMENT OBJECTIVE--Administrative assistant/executive secretary involving public contact, possible travel.

EMPLOYMENT HISTORY--
    1973 -- present
    Doctors Medical Group, Pasadena, Calif.
    Administrative assistant

    Manage billing office and supervise clerical staff of
    nine. Prepare financial statements, all tax returns,
    payroll, collections, and accounts receivable. Re-
    sponsible for administrative decisions.

SPECIAL ACCOMPLISHMENTS--
    . Established new accounting system which saved time and
      money.
    . Reduced accounts receivable delinquency rates.
    . Refined office procedures for greater efficiency.
    . Promoted to administrative assistant during first year
      of employment.

    1967-1973
    Tower Publishing Co. Los Angeles, Calif.
    Secretary to Marketing Manager

    Started as a secretary in the marketing department. Was
    promoted to secretary to manager of marketing. Respon-
    sibilities included telephone sales, proposal prepara-
    tion, and new business planning. Position required
    travel to New York and Boston for customer liaison.

SPECIAL ACCOMPLISHMENTS
    . Established new reporting system for field office per-
      sonnel which reduced "reporting in" time by 20%.
    . Designed format for letter proposals which improved
      efficiency and readability.
    . Served as marketing representative with three key
      clients, 1971-1973. Sales increased by 25% during
      that time.

EDUCATION
    University of Southern California, Los Angeles, Calif.
    Degree: Bachelor of Arts, 1966
    Major: English, Minor: Business

Figure 1-2
*A Sample Se-
quential Résumé.*

Leonard B. Byers   (date of résumé)
3759 Oaklane
Sierra Vista, Calif. 91001
694-3725

OBJECTIVE

Marketing management position from which to contribute to
company profitability and growth.

GENERAL QUALIFICATIONS

Marketing and business planning

Program organization and implementation

Engineering development and management

Communications - oral and written

Proposals and presentations

BUSINESS MANAGEMENT

Figure 1-3
A Sample Func-
tional Résumé.

Planned and managed administration, marketing, engineering,
and manufacturing for a new division of a diversified company. Evaluated company products and capabilities. Generated
viable business plans. Negotiated and committed internal
resources. Planned, coordinated, and implemented a new $2M
facility, including the acquisition of real property and
plant construction. Conducted cost/labor projections and
analyses.

MARKETING

Conceptualized new products. Developed new markets and
applications, resulting in $2.25M per year of additional
business. Performed market research and planning with cost-
weighted schedules to permit effective controls. Established
price structures and inventory controls. Conducted contract
negotiations. Established price structures and inventory
controls. Established and supervised East Coast sales representative network.

ENGINEERING

Directed systems engineering organization with a staff of
70 engineers and scientists. Generated program plans and
schedules. Guided project engineers toward goal achievement. Supervised test and operations department. Designed
and developed RF systems and components. Conducted vendor
negotiations.

Leonard B. Byers, Résumé (Continued)

FIRMS

1972 - present	Aerospace Products Inc., Los Angeles, California	Commercial products mgr.
1966 - 1972	Electronics, Inc. Van Nuys, California	Product line mgr.
1959 - 1966	Trans-Electronic Co. Boston, Mass.	Engineering mgr.

EDUCATION

Northeastern University, B.S. 1957, Major - Electronic Engineering

Northeastern University, M.S. 1959, Major - Business Management

PERSONAL DATA

Excellent health; married, three children.

can help him and his business before having a possible bias negate his objectivity. Hopefully, when he does finally see where all this marvelous experience was accumulated, he will be interested enough in the individual to talk to him anyway.

It is not just for ex-aerospace industry employees that the functional approach is effective. Anyone with broad experience over a number of years (and, perhaps, with a number of companies) can benefit from its use. Read the functional résumé of Leonard Byers (Figure 1-3) as though you were considering Mr. Byers for a job with your firm; does his résumé interest you enough so that you would want to meet with him?

Mr. Byers, with twenty years of experience, was able to get his entire résumé on a little over one page. In a way, this really is a summary résumé, and Mr. Byers can supply as much detail as required to support his statements. But the functional arrangement allows him to combine experience gained in management, whether at Aerospace Products or Electronics, Inc. It also provides valuable information early, before the reader is confronted with the aerospace background.

The résumé, incidentally, is real and was highly successful in getting interviews for Mr. Byers; he was hired by a small, expanding firm in the Los Angeles area to serve as director of international marketing.

Variations in Résumé Form

A slight variation on the functional résumé of Mr. Byers is the one presented in Figure 1-4. The applicant, Mr. Bledsoe, provides a brief section at the top entitled General Qualifications. He lists four areas: marketing and business planning, program management and control, financial planning and management, and proposal preparation and management. He follows this by using each general qualification as the heading for a brief discussion of specific accomplishments. This presentation directs the reader's eye to the sections the writer wants him to read in an order of priority selected by the writer.

There is an orderliness and parallelism to this résumé which gives it a professional air. The general qualifications perform the functions of outline headings but also tell the reader that this person is qualified to perform a variety of important management functions. Thus, the qualifications also serve as job objectives. Again, a well-experienced individual has been able to include key elements of his background in a one-page résumé.

This real résumé was sent initially to three selected companies. There was no reason to send out any more. All three companies (carefully screened first by Mr. Bledsoe) responded with interviews. Mr. Bledsoe is now a marketing manager for the first of the three companies to contact him.

Other variations on the functional résumé can be tailored by the individual to his own best features. A systems analyst, for example, designed his résumé in the form of a flowchart (see Figure 1-5). This layout might intrigue fellow analysts and very likely would get the attention of a personnel staffer. It accomplishes its purpose — to draw attention to the person and his skills. But, the flowchart presented in Figure 1-5 is really just an attention getter and would have to be accompanied by a complete résumé.

But there really is no need to go to extremes in the design of the résumé. A carefully structured page or two that emphasizes your strengths and, where practical, matches those strengths with the job requirements will suffice.

LETTERS OF APPLICATION

You have compiled a list of companies that are of interest to you and have done a preliminary screening of the list. You also have a file on yourself

LARRY R. BLEDSOE
100 Paso Real Ave.
Rowland Heights, Ca. 91748
(213) 964-4060

GENERAL QUALIFICATIONS

Marketing and business planning

Program management and control

Financial planning and management

Proposal preparation and management

MARKETING & BUSINESS PLANNING

Developed, monitored, and controlled product line/business plans for a major division of a medium-sized company. Prepared detailed business plans each year and monitored, controlled, and updated them each month. Also prepared 5-year business plans each year - and included market analysis, sales forecast, sales strategy and tactics, expected profit margins, and resource requirements.

PROGRAM MANAGEMENT & CONTROL

Managed R&D data processing programs ranging in value from $20,000 to $2,000,000, varying from 2-months to 18-months duration. Performed program scheduling, cost estimating, and control of these programs.

FINANCIAL PLANNING & MANAGEMENT

Recommended allocation of company discretionary resources (Bid & Proposal and IR&D funds) to top management. Monitored capital expenditures necessary to satisfy marketing objectives and performed ROI analysis for each business area.

PROPOSAL PREPARATION & MANAGEMENT

Involved in writing, organizing, and directing preparation of proposals for development of advanced data processing and sensor systems.

EDUCATION

M.B.A.	Business Administration	1971
M.S.	Electrical Engineering	1967
B.S.	Electrical Engineering	1964
B.S.	Mathematics	1963

FIRMS

1971 - 1974 Market Planning; Product Systems Co., Pomona, Ca.

1964 - 1971 Project Engineering; Jones Aircraft Co., Fullerton, Ca.

PERSONAL

Birth date: June 3, 1942

Figure 1-4
A Sample Variation of the Functional Résumé.

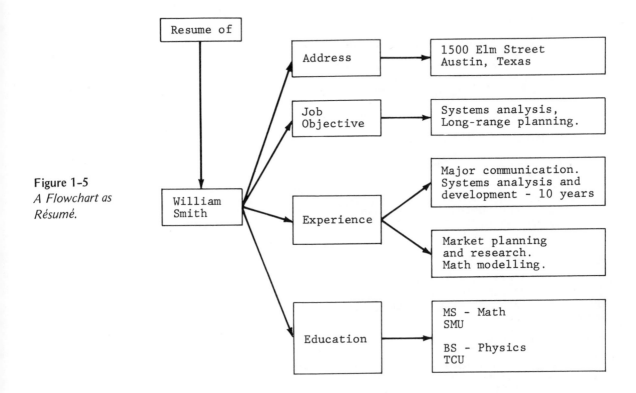

Figure 1-5
A Flowchart as Résumé.

and have prepared a résumé that is representative. You are now ready to send out the résumé with a letter of application.

Open Strongly

The letter of application is a sales letter. The product is you. Any good sales letter will first get the reader's attention. If you were to start your letter with, "Enclosed is my résumé; please review it and note my special experience with business machines and other office equipment," you have lost the battle before it gets a chance to start. First, by calling the reader's attention to the résumé in the first sentence, you are cuing the reader to go right to the résumé, thus negating the value of the letter. Second, there is no need to ask him to review it; he will get to it if he's interested in hiring someone. Third, and probably most damaging, is that this opening is bland, uninteresting, flat. Following are some opening sentences from application letters (some were accompanied by very fine résumés) which do nothing to help "sell" the writer. What is wrong with them?

Enclosed you will find a brief résumé of my experience and education regarding a position in. . .

Enclosed is a résumé of my work and experience qualifications.

Initially I would like to make a few comments about my personal and professional ambitions.

In researching the placement library of the university, I read of your company.

I will graduate from college in June with the degree of Bachelor of Science in Computer Sciences.

I am writing this letter with reference to future employment.

Unfortunately, most letters start off this way. The very valuable opening space of the letter, the place to attract the reader to you, is lost!

A better way to begin would be to associate a talent of yours with a requirement of his and to get some valuable information to him at the same time. The following sentences accomplish this. Contrast them with the preceding ones and note the differences.

Your advertisement of an opening for a secretary to assist designers of the first major oil northwest pipeline is one that really caught my attention.

As a black man with over ten years' experience in human relations management, I can help your company with programs concerning minorities. I have extensive experience in dealing with Affirmative Action and in establishing education and training courses.

I am a people-oriented secretary who has extensive administrative experience and who speaks fluent Spanish and French.

These openings say something. They provide interesting comments and are designed to attract attention to the letter itself before the reader turns to the résumé.

After the Opening, Then What?

After a *brief* opening paragraph designed to get attention and keep it, you should expand upon information in the résumé (but don't just repeat it).

If you have prepared a matrix and have identified the match-up areas, use that information to write the body of the letter. Stress the fact that your background matches the employer's requirements. The following section of an application letter does that.

> Several articles I have read indicate your company's interest in Computer Systems for Water Quality Control. While a student at Pasadena City College, I helped design a program for water quality control which had the unique feature of being adaptable to either fresh or salt water.

Ask yourself, "What have I done that this company would be interested in?" If you do not have any work experience that is applicable, stress school courses that would be of interest. Don't just list courses, since that information is on your résumé; describe something of interest that you did as a part of the course. For instance, if you are applying for a job as a technical writer and you took Report Writing in college, the fact that you took Report Writing should be on the résumé. In the letter you would say that in report writing you prepared a formal, technical report on the problem of instituting a rapid transit system in Cleveland, Ohio. Keep it brief but present enough to show the reader that you know what you're talking about.

Don't apologize for not having any experience; it may be an asset. Actually, don't apologize for anything: let the employer find out your weaknesses; don't provide him with a map.

You will, of course, be honest, direct, positive — and yet not overbearing. Be consistent in both tone and style, and make your letter reader oriented. In this way, you will avoid the number-one pitfall of application letters, the overuse of the pronoun "I." You can't avoid some I's, but don't make your letter one of those in which every sentence begins with "I."

How Do You Close the Letter?

Request something specific from the reader. Tell him you are available for an interview, can come to his office, or will be in town on a specific date. If you apply out of the state or country be sure you include a telephone number and an address where you can be reached. Don't just end blandly, like this:

> Thank you for your time and effort. Hope to hear from you soon.

Wouldn't it be more direct and positive to say:

> Please call me at 798–1450 to arrange an appointment. I will be pleased to discuss my plan for new business ventures with you.

This ending obviously refers back to a major point in the body of the letter and reinforces it. A conclusion that refers to a previously made point is always a good feature of sales letters and is effective here, too. You are not presenting a "hard sell"; you are just using the ending to re-establish your theme.

If travel is involved, you would naturally hope that the company will pay the expense. However, you could inquire as to whether there is an office or representative in your town with whom you could meet.

Figure 1–6 contains a sample letter of application that combines the features we have discussed:

1. Catchy, relevant beginning.
2. Supporting information.
3. You-orientation.
4. Confident tone, but not overbearing.
5. Amplification of the résumé, not just a repeat of it.
6. Positive ending.

PRACTICAL APPLICATIONS

Exercise 1. Seek Out Your Employer

Step 1. List the industries or businesses, (i.e., construction, transportation, banking, chemicals, teaching) you think you are interested in joining. Arrange them in a priority order. Briefly comment *why* you selected them.

1.
2.
3.
4.

                                        10250 Boulder Street
                                        Glendale, Ca. 90605
                                        April 1, 1975

Mr. Everett Doyle
Manager, Industrial Relations
Bellco Corporation
Los Angeles, Ca. 90601

Dear Mr. Doyle:

    To me, communications is the effective transmittal of ideas
from one person to another. My background and education have
helped to make me conscious of the need for effective communications at all levels of business. My degree in English and my
business background as legal secretary and administrative assistant prepare me well for a position on Bellco's writing staff.

Figure 1-6
A Sample Letter
of Application.

    As administrative assistant, I established a new reporting
procedure for a medium-size company in the medical supply field.
This procedure reduced the number of internal company reports
required over a six-month period from 125 to 55, at a savings of
$50,000. A special followup study conducted by a consultant
showed that communications is actually more effective because
of the elimination of overlapping and superfluous reports.

    In addition, I wrote, edited, and supervised the publica-
tions of weekly newsletters and quarterly news reports to
employees and clients.

    Please call me at 659-1050 or write to me and I will be
happy to discuss in more detail the cost-saving reporting system
and its possible application to Bellco communications.

                                        Sincerely,

                                        Sheila Archer

SA:ms
 Enclosure: Résumé

        5.
        6.
        7.
        8.
        9.
       10.

Step 2. Visit the library.

A. Consult at least three reference sources (Standard and Poor's *Industry Surveys; Industrial Marketing; The Occupational Outlook Handbook* are possibilities); read as much as you can find on trends, patterns, economical states of the top three or four industries you've selected. If still satisfied, leave the list as is; if not, rearrange the list and include new industries or businesses if it seems appropriate. Rearrange your new list, cut it after five entries, and comment on why there are changes from the previous list.

1.
2.
3.
4.
5.

B. Now select one industry to work within. Remember, if it does not turn out to be what you expected, you can come back to this list for selection No. 2 and so on.

C. Consult reference sources (*Career*, Moody's *Manuals*, Standard and Poor's *Manuals*) and select key companies in the industries you've chosen (up to 24). List the names of the companies. Arrange them as below — local (within 25 miles of your home), state, national, international. (If the headquarters or the division of the company that you will probably work for is located outside your local area, then list the company according to where that particular facility is located.)

Local
1.   4.
2.   5.
3.   6.

State
1.   4.
2.   5.
3.   6.

National

1.	4.
2.	5.
3.	6.

International

1.	4.
2.	5.
3.	6.

D. Select the companies you want to research. (The number depends upon your own interests and the amount of time you can spend on the project.) Read about them at the library: now consult trade journals, the periodical index, and periodicals such as *Fortune* (see if the company is listed in the Fortune 500), *Barrons, U.S. News and World Report, Business Week*. Take notes on the companies; list key features and names of key personnel, including the director of industrial relations or personnel, addresses, and any other information that seems pertinent.

Step 3. Send away for an annual report (or if one of your selected companies is local, visit it and pick up the report plus any other brochure or public relations material you can find). Keep an open file.

Exercise 2.   Prepare a File on Yourself

Step 1. List all your work experience.

Step 2. List all your education.

Step 3. List all relevant personal data.

Step 4. Design a preliminary résumé. Arrange the data compiled in the previous three steps in a *preliminary* résumé. Select either a format shown in Chapter 1 or one which fits your capabilities and experience.

Exercise 3.   Create a Matrix

You have a choice. You may prepare a matrix based on job opportunities you know about; or you may prepare one based on information set out in Chapter 2 on the Bellco Corporation. If you choose Bellco, you may apply for jobs in Marketing, Research and Development, Manufacturing, Industrial Relations and Personnel, or Publications. There are also a limited number of staff positions available, particularly in Public Relations and Finance. Before preparing your matrix, consult the sections in Chapter 2 which describe the department to which you want to apply. Then prepare your matrix according to the requirements of the department. Be sure to consult the Bellco organization chart (Figure 2-2) and the sample matrix in Chapter 1 (Figure 1-1).

Exercise 4. Design Your Résumé
Using the matrix you prepared in Exercise 3, do one of the following:

A. Prepare a general résumé not directed toward a specific job, but emphasizing your strengths as shown in the matrix.

B. Prepare a résumé directed toward a specific job opportunity that you know about.

C. Prepare a résumé directed toward a job opportunity at Bellco, as discussed in Exercise 3.

Exercise 5. Write the Letter of Application
Write a letter of application to accompany the résumé prepared in Exercise 4. Submit your matrix, letter of application, and résumé to your instructor.

THE COMPANY THAT HIRES
YOU - BELLCO ☞

2

Consider yourself a new employee of the Bellco Corporation. Bellco is a fictitious company the authors have created to provide an environment in which realistic memos, letters, proposals, and reports can be written. In this chapter you learn something about the current structure, communication policies, and personnel of the company. Do not think of it as a static organization. Like any other company trying to keep up with a competitive, fast-changing marketplace, Bellco needs change and improvement. Your ideas and suggestions, when presented in appropriate written or oral form, will be evaluated and, hopefully, adopted. Keep Bellco dynamic. Suggest changes in organization, products, markets, personnel, and communication policies.

WHAT IS BELLCO?

When A. D. Belliston started the Bellco Corporation in a garage in Pasadena, California, in 1947, he could little have realized that he was spawning a multimillion dollar conglomerate. It is not for us here to review the remarkable growth of this company; we are primarily concerned with its present status and in particular its methods of communications.

As a business enterprise, Bellco is of course interested in profits, earnings, sales, and expansion. However, the company has a social conscience, too; thus it emphasizes programs which attempt to improve the quality of life for all people.

How Current Programs Operate

The objective at Bellco is to combine a genuine feeling for humanity with good, practical business sense. Bellco will tackle anything that has potential to make easier our lot as participants in twentieth-century life. This breadth of interest can be readily seen by consulting Figure 2-1. While the list of programs is presented in a somewhat random order, you can make out the general areas of interest. If there are some you do not understand, no matter, set them aside for now. Certainly, you'll find someone at Bellco who will be able to enlighten you.

We do like to see a certain progression, a flow, at Bellco. It goes something like this. An idea is born, perhaps a thought on the way to work, or a light which blinks on in an employee's mind as he turns away from yet another TV commercial. New ideas are encouraged at Bellco. The idea is submitted to a new products committee which consists of representatives from the marketing and research and design departments. If the committee approves the idea, funds and personnel (from R & D) are assigned and the project is started. As the research progresses, the device, let's say it's a pocket computer, moves into preliminary design and development. Simultaneously, a market research and planning campaign is begun. The consumer market is sampled: Are there such devices already being sold? Who is the eventual customer? How much marketing is required? What is the market timing? As these two efforts — product development and market development — proceed, many checkpoints are established to ensure that the new computer has a reasonable chance for success. These checkpoints are usually associated with proof of progress. Thus, new funds may be withheld unless specific design goals are met. Progress reports and test results are presented periodically.

If the pocket computer is to be developed, then a pilot (limited) production line is established in the manufacturing department. A test-marketing program is often initiated concurrently. Perhaps Marketing will select New England as the area to be sampled. If all goes well in Marketing

Quality Environment Division

TO: R & D Writing Section   April 12, 1978

FROM: Carl Fujii

SUBJECT: List of Current Programs

The following list includes titles of all programs
currently under way:

Automated Postal Systems
Urban Parking Systems
Rail Rapid Transit Systems
Auto Emission Inspection Systems
Legislative Procedures for Reducing Pollutants
Rapid Transit to Suburban Areas (3 programs)
Growth of Recreational Areas
Rapid Transit in Pasadena as Model for L.A.
County
Low Cost Housing Units
Rapid Transit State-of-the-Art
Center City Rapid Transit (3 programs)
Educating Disadvantaged Youth
Leisure as Function of the State
Driver Training Programs
Traffic Control Systems
Four-Day Work Week
Computer Systems for Water Quality Control
Computer Systems for Downtown Traffic Control
Handwriting Optical Interpreting Systems
Mathematical Models for Ecosystems
Hydrogen as New Energy Source
Belltowers - Use of Airspace over Freeways
Smog Reduction Systems
Commuter Bicycle System
Fluidic Control of Communication Systems
Computer Systems for Shopping From the Home
Elements of Atmospheric Pollution
Greenbelt Planning
Automated Computer Market Checkout System

Figure 2-1
*Current Programs
at Bellco.*

and Manufacturing, then production lines can be set up, and the computer
will be mass produced, or at least produced in numbers commensurate
with Marketing's sales projections.

Of course this is a mere sketch of a process that could take anywhere
from three to five years, but it is the "cradle-to-grave" approach (that is,

an approach that accounts for every phase of the production, from idea to marketed product) that is favored at Bellco. To ensure that a high percentage of ideas germinate into profit-bearing products, good communications is a necessity. At Bellco, this means effective, direct, "tell-it-like-it-is" communications.

In keeping with the objective of producing products that improve the quality of life, Mr. Belliston formed the Quality Environment Division (QED). It is with the activities of this division that you, as a communicator and now an employee of the company, will be concerned. The QED has a "cradle-to-grave" capability of its own: it, too, has the personnel and facilities to design, develop, produce, and market products. Certainly, the division can call on Bellco corporate support when it needs to; but except perhaps for assistance in public relations and finance, it is unlikely to do so.

The QED operates as a small company within the complex of Bellco companies. James Burke, the director of the division, has a streamlined organization which emphasizes line functions. At Bellco, line departments are those directly responsible for getting the job done; staff personnel are primarily advisory. As shown in the organization chart, Figure 2-2, Mr. Burke has only one staff executive reporting to him, Chandra Wilson, the controller. All others reporting to Mr. Burke are managers of line departments. The five line departments are the basic elements of the QED: marketing; research and development; manufacturing (which includes production); industrial relations and personnel; and publications.

HOW DOES BELLCO WORK?

So that you, the new employee, may see how the company operates, let us briefly examine the departments and their functions. For our purposes, the QED is Bellco Corporation, and the names are used interchangeably.

Marketing

This department provides contact with the customer. At Bellco, no one, not even Mr. Belliston, speaks to a customer without Marketing's knowledge and, in most cases, concurrence. Any employee who is in contact with a customer is required to report the contact to Marketing, in writing, immediately upon concluding the contact. All written correspon-

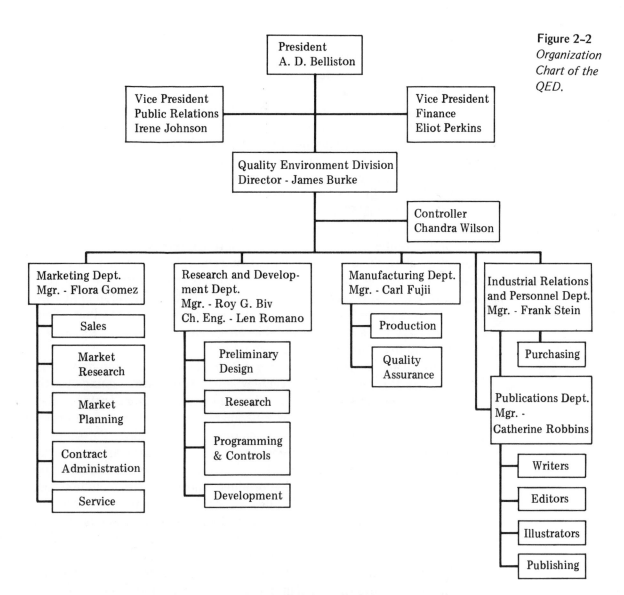

Figure 2-2
*Organization
Chart of the
QED.*

dence with customers or potential customers should originate within or be approved by Marketing. Thus, if you end up as a member of the research and development department and it happens that a customer requests you to describe a product, you should write the response but get Marketing approval before mailing it.

Marketing is organized in five sections: sales, market planning, market research, contract administration, and service. Each section has separate responsibilities for developing and maintaining customer satisfaction and for increasing customer confidence in the company and its products.

The sales section has the primary responsibility for selling the company's products. It consists of outside salespersons, including district offices, and inside (telephone) salespersons. Outside sales personnel call on customers, try to find and develop new customers, and alert the company to potential customer relations problems. They operate out of the QED's main facility in Los Angeles but spend better than 50 percent of their time traveling. They are also responsible for coordinating all district office activities. District offices are located in all major cities throughout the United States and in selected cities internationally. The district office personnel alert Sales to potential customer problems and help direct the visiting salesperson to possible new customers. By working as a part of Sales, district offices ensure a coordinated customer development campaign. Should a problem arise with one of the division's products, Sales alerts the service section to provide an expert promptly to service the product and maintain customer satisfaction.

The Bellco crystal ball resides within the market planning section. Personnel in this section help decide where the company is going over the next one to ten years and how it will get there. This scheme includes planning for new products, for new customers, and for new and improved facilities. Market Research works closely with Planning. Personnel in Market Research are primarily concerned with how the marketplace will greet a new Bellco product and with what can be done about making the marketplace more receptive to that product. Their activities include setting up market research programs for new products, sampling various sections of the country for customer response to Bellco and its products, and statistical analysis of test results to ensure maximum sales and profitability.

Contract Administration is primarily concerned with the legal implications of the business. Contracts with customers and suppliers are monitored to ensure that all clauses are met. Personnel in Contract Administration conduct negotiations on follow-on (i.e., additions to existing contracts) and new business contracts, and they write and process the documentation.

Service section personnel maintain and repair Bellco products. Since they have frequent customer contact, they are a part of the marketing department. In this way, customer complaints can be immediately funneled to Sales and Contract Administration for attention. Hopefully, by prompt attention to the problem, the service section will be able to satisfy a Bellco customer well enough that he will remain a Bellco customer.

Research and Development

The work conducted in this department is the key to Bellco's growth and continuing status as a leader in industry. The three sections of R & D work closely together to guard against overlap and to ensure that "good" ideas become profitable products.

Preliminary designers develop the design requirements, or criteria, that specify precisely the (a) configuration, (b) materials, and (c) performance standards of each part, component, assembly, subsystem, and system produced.

Research specialists investigate "the state of the art," or current technology, so that they keep up to date on what can be done with various materials, methods, processes, and techniques to meet the designer's requirements. They evaluate new developments and develop new materials and methods themselves. They keep busy on two fronts: meeting immediate design requirements and contributing to the state of the art.

Development engineers take over the design requirements when the other two sections have completed their work. First the engineers build a "mockup," or model, to the requirements for configuration; then they set out to construct an optimum prototype — one that meets the design requirements at a cost the company can afford. It may be that to build the optimum prototype the development engineers will have to develop new materials and new manufacturing methods to make production more profitable. But their main job as they build the prototype is to develop detailed "specifications," or instructions, on how to produce the product so that it conforms to the design requirements: how each part must be built; what materials must be used; and what tests must be given to every part, component, assembly, subsystem, and system before it is acceptable.

Manufacturing

When the prototype has been developed and tested, the new product is ready for production. It goes to the factory. The factory workers must follow the specifications, which may appear as "specs," blueprints, schematics, or manuals. Any departure from these specifications must be done by the preliminary design section, because one slight change could affect other parts. Quality control inspectors throughout the factory check the product at every stage of manufacturing to ensure that all specifications are being met. Computerized systems keep records of each part throughout the production process and sometimes throughout its service life. In this way, Bellco learns whether their specifications are right. If anyone sees that a specification can be improved, he informs the preliminary designers, who then work it out. Meanwhile, everyone works to the original specifications until they are changed.

Industrial Relations and Personnel

Some of the activities in I R & P are: hiring, firing, promoting, negotiating with labor, conducting management development programs, providing employee benefit packages, and planning and implementing special events. While requisitions for new hires originate in the requesting department, it is Personnel that places ads, screens résumés and letters of application, and conducts first-level interviews. The department is responsible for operating Bellco's Affirmative Action program, a model for industry.

Publications

Writers, editors, and illustrators provide all kinds of informational services to the company as a whole. They may be called upon by designers or R & D engineers to prepare specifications or instructions. They often write reports for these departments as well as for Manufacturing. But most of their time is taken up by the marketing department. They prepare proposals for new business, brochures, and other sales literature. They write original copy or may be called upon to edit, synopsize, or organize written material prepared elsewhere in the company. Final editing, illustrating, and publication of all company reports, proposals, and sales literature is the responsibility of Publications.

WHO IS BELLCO?

It may be trite, but it's true: Bellco's success is due to the excellence of its personnel. From the highest tiers of management to the workers in the plant, the company strives for teamwork. As a new employee, you will be working and communicating with a group of experienced business people. You will want to have some idea as to their background and experience, so let's look at some brief biographical sketches.

These personnel sketches are included so that you can learn about:

1. The management personnel at Bellco.
2. How a general biographical sketch is written.

If you were given the assignment to write a paragraph or two on a Bellco employee for use in a proposal or annual report, chances are you would describe his background by using one of the following formats:

a. Education
   Experience prior to Bellco
   Experience at Bellco
   Current position, duties, and responsibilities

b. Current position, duties, and responsibilities
   Other Bellco work
   Experience prior to Bellco
   Education (optional)

c. Experience prior to Bellco
   Experience at Bellco
   Current position, duties, and responsibilities
   Education (optional)

At Bellco, the preferred format is (b). Management feels that the reader is most interested in what employees are doing *now*, so they want that information to be first. An employee's other experience, at Bellco and elsewhere, should be supportive; and his or her education is of interest only in support of the individual's current position and responsibilities. When the education background is routinely presented at the end of the sketch, then it is an easy matter to leave it out entirely. It should be included only if you feel that it enhances the background of the subject.

The writing should be informal, even personal, without being intimate. Write about the person so that the reader sees him as a person competent in his job. Biographical sketches are minirésumés.

A. D. Belliston, President. As president and chief executive officer of the company, Mr. Belliston is active in its day-to-day supervision and is a strong believer in management development programs. Because of his efforts in this area, most of Bellco's management personnel have come up through the ranks. He feels that a successful company should maintain a balance between marketing established products and developing new products. Prior to starting Bellco, Mr. Belliston was head of product design and development for General Electric. He has a BSEE degree from the California Institute of Technology.

Irene Johnson, Vice President, Public Relations. As director of public relations, Mrs. Johnson is responsible for the Bellco image. She has supervision over all releases to the media and maintains close contact with local, national, and international news sources. Recent Bellco innovations have received first-page coverage in newspapers across the country because of the diligence of Mrs. Johnson and her staff. She formerly worked on the editorial staff of the *New York Times* and attended Columbia University School of Journalism.

Eliot Perkins, Vice President, Finance. As vice president of finance, Mr. Perkins's primary responsibility is to keep the balance sheet balanced. He keeps close watch on expenditures and revenues and is known to project the attitude of "sell me on it first" before he will commit funds to a new project. He recognizes the optimism and enthusiasm of marketing personnel but insists that solid development and marketing plans be prepared and implemented before major commitments of funds are made. He has been with Bellco for 17 years, starting as an accountant in the QED. He is a graduate of Sawyer.

James Burke, Director, QED. It is commonly agreed that Mr. Burke is the busiest person at Bellco. As division director, he is responsible for all activities of the division — including marketing, product development, manufacturing, and production. Formerly, as head of manufacturing at Bellco, he developed an automated production line which incorporated advanced computer technology yet provided for frequent, individual inspection of parts. The system was praised by both union and management personnel as being efficient and productive. Mr. Burke has been with Bellco since its inception and came to the company after receiving his A.A. degree in engineering at Los Angeles City College.

Chandra Wilson, Controller. The controller does just that, controls the money of the QED. Ms. Wilson was hand picked by Mr. Perkins and maintains a direct influence on all funding. She was responsible for the development of the "flash report" — a weekly, one-page report on the division's financial status which goes to Mr. Perkins and Mr. Belliston. The report summarizes the division's expenditures, sales, and profits for the period. Ms. Wilson worked for an accounting firm in the Washington, D.C., area following her graduation from Howard University.

Flora Gomez, Manager, Marketing. When Ms. Gomez took over the marketing department, sales were down, profit had gone negative, and growth potential seemed nonexistent. She immediately set about rehabilitating the department. She began by examining product lines and dropping nonprofit items. A market survey revealed untapped market areas, and Ms. Gomez began programs to exploit these. She instituted new incentive programs the first year which sparked great enthusiasm among the salespeople. Under her leadership, commissions were increased for some field sales personnel, and more effective avenues of communication were instituted among all marketing personnel. In one year, sales and profits climbed. Ms. Gomez was sales manager for Marvel Toys before coming to Bellco. She has an MBA from UCLA.

Roy G. Biv, Manager, Research and Development. Mr. Biv is responsible for selecting research projects and for processing them through development and into production. Mr. Biv is noted for his originality and inventiveness. It is his type of creative originality which inspires his employees and gives R & D its enviable record. Since Mr. Biv joined Bellco, 75 percent of the products processed through R & D have gone into production. Prior to joining Bellco, he served as U.S. Director for Energy Research for five years; he was a consultant to oil and gas companies on the feasibility of the Alaskan pipeline and he was selected by President Nixon to represent this country in international energy discussions. He attended the University of Chicago and Northwestern University.

Len Romano, Chief Engineer, R & D. As chief engineer, Mr. Romano works closely with engineering personnel on all new products in R & D. He "troubleshoots" specific engineering problems and assigns engineering personnel to ongoing projects. Mr. Romano's background is in aerodynamics and aircraft design. He has worked at the Ames Research Center,

Moffet Field, California, and at the California Institute of Technology's Jet Propulsion Lab in Pasadena. At both facilities he was responsible for wind tunnel research on swept-wing design aircraft. He has a BS from Alabama University.

Carl Fujii, Manager, Manufacturing. If there is one thing that Mr. Fujii does especially well, and there are many, it is to get along with his workers in the factory. He is often seen there, sleeves rolled up, working alongside the lathe and drill press operators. No job is too large or too small for Mr. Fujii. At one time or another in his career, he has worked on each of the machines used in manufacturing. From this experience, he learned not only about the safe and effective operation of machinery, but also about the importance of the worker as an individual. He has been able to apply this experience effectively as manager of manufacturing.

Frank Stein, Manager, Industrial Relations and Personnel. At Bellco, personnel and industrial relations are important — critical — departments. Mr. Stein, as manager, is the primary reason why employees tend to stay and grow with the company. He is careful in selecting new employees, but then takes care that they are given every opportunity to develop and move into positions of greater authority and responsibility. He was selected Personnel Manager of the Year by Harvard Business School because of his work in implementing management development programs.

Catherine Robbins, Manager, Publications. Ms. Robbins has built an effective, versatile staff of writers, editors, and artists who are responsible for many publications of Bellco: brochures, proposals, reports, pamphlets, presentation materials, and journal articles. Prior to coming to Bellco, she worked for small publishing companies on the West Coast. Her book, *Writing in Industry*, is widely used in schools, industry, and government.

PRACTICAL APPLICATIONS

Exercise 1. Write a Personnel Memo
You work for Ms. Robbins and she has asked you to write a memo to Mrs. Johnson in Public Relations, supplying her with essential information on key Bellco personnel. Mrs. Johnson intends to release the informa-

tion you have prepared, as part of a feature story on Bellco, to newspapers around the country. Select essential information from the sketches presented in this chapter; you may add any additional information that you possess on the personnel involved. (That is, because this is a fictitious company, the "files" you consult for supplemental information are, of course, only in your head. Be inventive, but be reasonable — and not silly. The purpose of this exercise is to see if you can select and appropriately write up the significant facts in a personnel memo.) Check the memo presented as Figure 2-1 for the correct form.

Exercise 2. Write an Operations Report

Examine the list of current programs, Figure 2-1. Prepare a brief, one-page memo addressed to James Burke. On the subject line write "Operations Report." Mr. Burke has asked you to group the apparently disparate programs under headings and possibly subheadings which will make it easier for him to categorize activities. You make up the headings. If you decide that Rapid Transit Systems might be a good heading, which programs would you list under it? Programs that you are not sure about or that do not seem to fit in any particular category may be placed in an Other or Miscellaneous column.

Exercise 3. Draw Up a Production Timetable

Think of a new product, one you've always wished existed, or one you think is forthcoming: perhaps a lock that glows in the dark so you can insert your key easily; a solar-powered car or solar-heated house; an economical method to desalinate sea water. Draw up a functional timetable of events for your idea from inception to production. What steps do you think Bellco should take to help ensure the success of your idea? What steps can you take? What should Marketing do? How can Ms. Gomez help you? Do not be concerned about funds; just list those steps that you think the company would logically take to see your product through development and into production, and assign dates to the steps (month/year only). Compare your product development timetable with others in the class. Is yours realistic?

Exercise 4. Work Up a Policy Program

In the section in this chapter on Industrial Relations and Personnel, the statement is made that Bellco has an Affirmative Action program.

Research Affirmative Action in the library and at companies near your school. What is it? How is it supposed to function? After gathering as much information as you can, consult Part Two, the Troubleshooter's Guide; it will give you some tips on how to organize, plan, outline, and rough-draft a specific Affirmative Action program for Bellco.

The rough draft should be read and critiqued by the class or a committee selected by the class. After approval, it should be typed up as a Bellco Affirmative Action policy statement.

(Note: This exercise may be done by one student or by a group of students who form an Affirmative Action policy development committee.)

THE BUSINESS LETTER 3

Most of us feel that we can be persuasive in a face-to-face encounter. We receive immediate feedback during a conversation and can adjust to that feedback. But when we pick up a pen to write we often write stilted prose, which is not just unlike our real selves: it is a barrier to effective communication. Why shouldn't we write letters the way we carry on conversations?

In this chapter we are going to look at what it is that makes a good business letter. We shall consider the types of letters, according to their intent, and the basic elements needed to make a letter effective. Finally, we shall look at ways to check a letter for readability.

TYPES OF BUSINESS LETTERS, BY INTENT

Business letters are usually categorized by what they are intended to do. There are collection, credit, claim, adjustment, inquiry, order, sales, and persuasive letters. Each letter is expected to achieve a purpose. It is up to the writer to decide how to achieve the purpose. For instance, if you, a business person, have an excellent credit rating and are interested in buying on credit from a supplier, it is probably enough for you to state this fact early and directly in your credit request letter. On the other hand, if you've had trouble recently meeting your commitments and your credit rating has suffered, then you have some explaining to do before you go blithely ahead asking for credit. You will want to establish your case in a reasonable, logical manner before making your request. You're assuming that a reasonable, logical person will read your letter and will react accordingly.

It is not the intent of this chapter to describe in detail each type of business letter and to provide a form or model for each. Rather, it will describe an approach that can be applied to all types of business letters.

THE BASIC QUESTIONS

Before you start writing, you should take a few minutes to plan and prepare, to set up the letter. To do this, ask yourself six questions and jot down your responses. The six questions are:

1. To whom am I writing?
2. What is my purpose?
3. What is my theme?
4. Should my letter be up-front or a convincer?
5. What are my key points?
6. What action do I want the reader to take?

This process shouldn't take long. The six questions pertain to any business letter you may be called upon to write. They are ordered logically, but the order can be varied to suit your own writing habits. The idea is to get pertinent information on paper so that you have the choice of what to include and what to exclude. The questions and answers will help to keep you from forgetting something important, and should help you keep your letter on a conversational level.

Let's examine the six questions individually and see how the setting-up process can actually make letter writing easier and more efficient and effective.

To Whom Am I Writing?

In business writing, just as in a business meeting, the more you know about the person to whom you are writing or speaking, the easier it should be to communicate your ideas to him. How well do you know your reader? What are his likes, dislikes? What business transactions took place with him in the past? Is he a personal friend of anyone in the company?

Suppose you know nothing about the recipient. This is often the case in "cold-turkey" sales letters, those sent to people on mailing lists. You may have some statistical data on the population that composes the mailing list — such as the ratio of males to females, or the number of senior citizens, or the economic range it represents. Use whatever information you have available to you. If you have no information on the recipients, state that as your answer to Question 1 and go on to Question 2.

What Is My Purpose?

Another way to phrase this question is: What am I trying to accomplish? Be specific in your answer: it is not just to collect on an overdue bill; it is to collect $4500 from James Dunn for spare parts shipped to him six months ago. The purpose is a part of your notes and does not go into the letter itself. It should be kept in front of you, though, to remind you of your goal and to minimize digressions. When you have finished the letter and read it over to yourself, reread your purpose statement. Does the letter appear to you to address the purpose? Is it on target?

What Is My Theme?

If your purpose is to collect the $4500 from Mr. Dunn, your theme might very well be that Mr. Dunn's credit rating will suffer greatly if he doesn't pay up. This theme can be repeated at strategic points throughout the letter to remind him that a businessman without credit is like a shark without teeth.

Recurring themes are especially effective in persuasive and sales letters. If you're trying to sell a lawnmower and your key sales feature is that it cuts grass flush against fences, walls, or sidewalks, thus eliminating the need for a separate edger, then make that your theme. State it in the first paragraph and mention it again at key points throughout the letter. Remind the reader again in the last paragraph, too. If he remembers nothing else from your letter, he'll picture your mower cutting right up against his fence; and the next time he goes out to mow his lawn and sees the grass growing over the sidewalk or shooting up long blades next to the garage, he may feel that it's time to invest in your product.

While the theme may dominate the letter, it is not the only feature described. You mention the other features too; it's just that you feel that the feature you've selected for your theme is the most likely one to interest new buyers. Your letter on a lawnmower with the flush-cut feature (let's call it the Omnimower) might start like this:

> Dear Homeowner,
>
> You've just finished mowing your lawn with your old mower; you're tired and ready for a cold beer. But wait, there it is again, that same old shaggy grass along the edges of your lawn. You go back to the garage and drag out the edger; there's more work to be done.
>
> Familiar story? No more. Not with Omnimower. Now, in one step, you can have a beautifully manicured lawn throughout, right up to the fence, or wall, or sidewalk; no more shag!
>
> Omnimower cuts it all!

You've established your theme early. Another mention of it in the middle of the letter and again at the end should reinforce it. The statement in the last paragraph might read:

> And Omnimower does it all in one step — cuts high grass, low grass, and all that hard-to-get-at-grass along the edges. . . .

Should My Letter Be Up-Front or a Convincer?

The difference between an up-front letter and a convincer is how much persuasion you think is required to convince the reader to take the action you want him to take. If very little persuasion is required, an up-front letter will do. Just say what it is you have to say early in the letter. If not — if the reader must be convinced — then develop your case logically to a conclusion your reader will agree with.

After you have jotted down information about the reader, your purpose in writing to him, and your theme or motif, you will probably know whether you will want to write an up-front letter or a convincer. Most inquiries, information letters, and affirmative credit letters will be up-front letters. In fact, most letters saying what the reader wants to hear will be up-front letters. When you have good news for someone, you don't hold it back; you blurt it out early in the conversation. Do the same with a letter that provides good news.

The Up-Front Letter. The up-front letter is one that tells the reader what he needs to know in the first and second paragraphs. The rest of the letter, if more is required, supplies supporting details. For instance, suppose that Mr. Belliston asked you to draft a letter for him, to get a business acquaintance to come out to observe a new production technique. You write:

> Dear Mr. Berne,
>   We're finally having that open house I talked to you about. Our new automated production line, which interested you so much, will be on display and operating in our Los Angeles facility. Mary (Mrs. Belliston) and I are expecting you and Mrs. Berne to be our guests for the three days, February 12–15th.

That's easy enough. You've written the first paragraph and, like a newspaper story, you've answered the questions: who, what, when, where, and why. Now you can fill out the rest of the letter for Mr. Belliston with whatever details you think are necessary. You did not expect any problems in accomplishing your purpose because you knew that Mr. Berne was already motivated to attend the open house. Thus, you were able to launch right into the purpose of the letter, the invitation, in the very first paragraph and to write it conversationally, just as if Mr. Belliston were speaking to him.

The Convincer. In the previous example, you invited a customer to an open house, knowing that he was already inclined to come. Suppose that a Mr. Congdon, who lives in New York, hates to travel and needs some convincing before he will make the trip to the open house. He's a good customer, and you know the new production line will be of great interest to him, because he's been needling the company over inefficiency in production methods. Now Bellco engineers feel that this new facility greatly enhances their efficiency.

Mr. Belliston has explained this background on Mr. Congdon to you, and he has asked that you write a draft letter to this customer too. He doesn't use the terms "convincer" and "up-front," but you understand from his description of Mr. Congdon that you will need to be more persuasive. You know this situation calls for a convincer rather than an up-front letter:

Dear Mr. Congdon,

No one thought it possible, but it's working. A new automated production line is now turning out 20,000 chips a day (the best we did with the old line was 7500). Not only have we increased production, but quality is up too — less than 1% rejection with the new line; over 5% with the old one. And you are the benefactor.

You may see the new line in operation; see your product as it proceeds through the fully automated system, watch as it is electronically scanned and inspected, and catch it as it drops into your hand at the end of the line.

Come to the open house at Bellco on February 12–15th. . . .

You decided that Mr. Congdon needed some good, friendly persuasion. You know that he is interested in efficiency, and in his product, so you gave them prominence in your letter by devoting the first two paragraphs to them. The actual invitation now doesn't come until the third paragraph, until you feel that Mr. Congdon is convinced that it might be a very good thing, indeed, if he took a trip to California to see this new system in operation. The convincer differs from the up-front letter because it prepares the reader first, before requesting action. However, like the up-front letter, it is conversational in tone.

What Are My Key Points?

Make a list of those points you think you might want to include in the letter. Do not be concerned about order, spelling, or grammar. Initially you want as complete a list as you can compile. After you are satisfied that you have jotted down everything that comes to mind, pare the list and eliminate items you know you can't use. Then list the remaining items in priority so that you can be sure to give the key points proper emphasis in the letter.

For instance, if you are trying to write a sales letter on a new ten-speed bicycle, the Omnicycle, the initial list might include such items as:

economy of operation
weight — 30 lbs.
lugged fittings for added rigidity
wide gear range, 33–100
rear derailleur gearing system
ease of shifting
auxiliary brake levers
competitive price, $135.00
pedal crank bearings sealed to protect from road grit
comes in racer model only
comfortable saddle seat

You would be trying to cram too much into a single letter if you attempted to include all of the preceding points. Be selective. Cross out all but the key items and give those a priority:

2. economy of operation
3. weight — 30 lbs.
     ~~lugged fittings for added rigidity~~
1. wide gear range, 33–100
     ~~rear derailleur gearing system~~
     ~~ease of shifting~~
4. auxiliary brake levers
5. competitive price, $135.00
     ~~pedal crank bearings sealed to protect from road grit~~
     ~~comes in racer model only~~
     ~~comfortable saddle seat~~

Now you have five items to work with in your letter. Item number 1 is the theme and should agree with the theme already selected for the letter. In this case, the wide gear range of 33–100 is the best selling point and is the theme of the letter and the point emphasized throughout. Item 2, economy of operation, can also be treated as a theme and reinforced throughout the letter. But no more than 1 or 2 items can function effectively this way. The other points will be presented in a supporting fashion.

How do you select the theme? (In this case, why choose the wide gear range?) One reason could be that competitive bicycles in that price range feature gearing systems that go from 39 to 90. Thus, the Omnicycle provides better hill-climbing capability (the lower gear ranges do this) and easier pedaling and perhaps more speed on the straightaways (the higher gear ratio).

To give your key points more emphasis in the letter and to make them come alive, put your reader in the picture and make him active with the product. Put him on the bicycle. Let him experience riding it up hills, down hills, on straightaways, along an ocean pathway. What would you say to the client to convince him to buy your product if you were speaking to him? Imagine it, then write your letter that way.

If you decide that economy is an equally good selling point and that it should by your theme instead, or act as your complementary theme, you will have to be more specific. Why does this bike mean economy to the buyer: Is there a better warranty than competitors offer? Is the maintenance easier? Do you provide a repair kit and manual with the bike? The answers to these questions would tell you whether economy is a strong enough selling point to function as a theme.

What Action Do I Want the Reader to Take?

This is the last and probably most crucial (and often most neglected) question to ask. The reader must be given something specific to do. Effective sales letters include a response card (filled in except for the customer's signature) to make it as easy as possible for the customer to order the product. In a letter of inquiry, be sure to include a proper address to which the material should be sent. If timing is crucial to you, then be sure to say so: "I need the material by February 14th."

Try to be as specific as you can. When you're preparing the list in preparation for writing the letter, respond to the questions in concrete terms; i.e., give dates, quantities, amounts, times, places. "I will meet you at 9 AM, August 14th, in my office at 1400 Wilshire Blvd., Los Angeles. If this is not convenient, call me at 213/744-3100, ext. 270, for another appointment." This sentence might very well conclude a letter written in response to a letter of application. The action you request must be commensurate with the letter itself. You do not want to demand action at the conclusion to a sales letter; you want to make it so easy for the receiver of the letter to take action that it becomes nearly reflexive for him to do.

THE OPTIONS ARE YOURS

As the writer, you hold all the options. You can make the letter strong or weak, active or passive, flowery or direct, pleasant or unpleasant. You make the decisions as to tone, style, language (that is, level of vocabulary, whether you use business or technical terms, etc.), and approach. The six questions provided here are a guideline; they cover basic information required in virtually all business letters. It is your decision as to how thoroughly you wish to apply them. For a routine letter, you may just want to skim down the list, jot down some quick notes to yourself, and commence writing right away. The whole process could take less than a minute. However, when you first begin to use the list, you should apply it well, even for routine letters. The more familiar you are with its application, the better it works for you.

TEST YOUR LETTER FOR EFFECTIVENESS

The ultimate test for the effectiveness of your letter is the reader's response. But, before you receive that, there are three things you can do to help assure yourself that you've done the best job possible.

1. Read the letter and, as you do, ask yourself the six questions. Have you considered who the reader is? Is the theme clear? Have you chosen the right type of letter, up-front or convincer? Are all the key points included? Do you have an action ending? Do you achieve your purpose?

2. Read the letter aloud, preferably to a fellow worker. Does it sound all right? Often by reading a letter aloud, we hear discordances that do not show up in a silent scan.

3. Proofread it carefully for misspellings and typographical errors. Did you spell the customer's name right? His organization? Is his address correct?

TRYING OUT THE SYSTEM

Let's take a problem and work it through together. Ms. Gomez, the marketing manager, has asked you to write a letter to Roger Brown, president of Save the Environment, Inc., a retail company that sells only products designed to improve the environment. Mr. Brown's company has been the single largest purchaser of the Omnicycle, the ten-speed bicycle that Bellco makes. The bicycle was new last year; but since then, competition among manufacturers has increased, and there are now many good ten-speed bikes on the market, at competitive prices. You are to write a letter to Mr. Brown extolling the features of the new Omnicycle. You know that Mr. Brown is getting ready to purchase the next year's models. Start with the six questions and fill in the information available. Then try to write a letter which uses that information.

To Whom Am I Writing?

> Mr. Roger Brown, President
> Save the Environment, Inc.
> 2775 West 35th Street
> New York, N.Y. 10036

Young (33), aggressive, a no-nonsense type, likes to have facts to go on, a doer, comes to the point quickly, all business, very, very serious about cleaning up the environment. Formerly worked for Ralph Nader. Thinks well of Bellco products, good customer last year, bought 5,000 Omnicycles.

What Is My Purpose? To convince Mr. Brown to continue buying Omnicycles.

What Is My Theme? There are two themes:

1. Omnicycle sold well for Mr. Brown last year and now has an entirely new feature, derailleur shift positions, to make it even more desirable.
2. Use of the Omnicycle by more people instead of perhaps a second car would result in a cleaner environment.

Should My Letter Be Up-front or a Convincer? Convincer; but keep it short. Mr. Brown likes to have the facts.

What Are My Key Points?

Priority

theme	*1*	Omnicycle very popular throughout U.S., selling well and helping environment, no emissions.
theme	*1*	New gearing system on next year's model. Rider now has shift positions (1–10) clearly indicated on shift levers.
old feature		Lugged joints for rigidity
old		33–100 derailleur
new	*2*	Weight reduced to 28 lbs. (previously 30 lbs.)
old, but important	*7*	Price stays the same at $135.00 retail. Price to Mr. Brown, $75.00.
new	*3*	Slightly wider seat for more comfort
old	*5*	Lifetime frame warranty
old	*6*	One-year overall warranty
old		~~Auxiliary brake levers~~
old		~~Sealed pedal crank bearings~~
new	*4*	Unisex design

What Action Do I Want Him to Take? I am not asking him to place an order now; that will come in response to our proposal next month. I want to convince him of two things: that Omnicycle is the bike to buy; to meet with me in New York next week. Considering all the preceding information, the letter might read as in Figure 3–1. Test this letter for effectiveness. Does it take the reader into account? Is the purpose achieved? What key points are included; what points are excluded? Why do you think the writer did not include more of the bicycle's features? Test this letter with the Fog Index readability formula explained in the following section.

CHECK YOUR READABILITY LEVEL

This book emphasizes writing concisely, clearly, correctly, and convincingly. It also shows you how to adjust your writing to your reader. How can you, the writer, know whether you have done these things? True, there is a certain intuitive feel that some writers seem to have which tells them that what they've written is appropriate. But not all of us are blessed with this kind of intuition. Is there anything else? Is there a way to measure a passage of writing to determine the clarity and the reading level of the

Mr. Roger Brown, President
Save the Environment, Inc.
2775 West 35th Street
New York, N.Y. 10036

Dear Mr. Brown:

The all-new Omnicycles will soon be coming off the assembly lines. They should sell even better this year than last for
two basic reasons: (1) The Omnicycle has some new features that
will make cycling easier and more attractive to more people.
(2) More Americans are environment-conscious now; they have
stopped talking environment improvement and are doing something
about it. Sales of ten-speeds are expected to increase by 50
percent over last year.

The most impressive improvement on this year's Omnicycle
is the 10-position shifting lever. It takes the guesswork out
of shifting; now the rider knows immediately what gear he or
she is in. Each position is clearly marked and notched on the
lever itself. Surveys show that many people are reluctant to
try 10-speeds because of the uncertainty in shifting. Well, the
Omnicycle makes that uncertainty a thing of the past.

In addition, we have been able to reduce the bike's weight
to 28 lbs. from last year's 30 lbs. by going to a new alloy,
Bellcosteel, which is even more rugged than previous alloys
used. We have also improved the seat by using a tensioned
leather design and by making it wider for more riding comfort.

Another new feature is the new unisex model which makes
no sexist distinctions. The unisex model has all the features
of the other models but instead of a bar across the top, as
in male bicycles, it has two sturdy tubes running from the
steering head to the rear axle. In tests recently completed,
this design proved to be as rugged as the top tube designs
and had the added advantage of providing ease of mounting and
dismounting. The new model is pictured in the enclosed brochure
on page 4.

You are familiar with the remaining features of the current
bike. These will all be continued - including the life-time
warranty on the frame and the one-year warranty on all parts.
Most astonishing of all, Mr. Brown, is that because of new,
more efficient production processes, we can keep the wholesale
price at $75.00/each, in spite of the improvements and the
pressures of inflation.

To us at Bellco, bicycling is an important answer to air
pollution. Our designers are conscious of the need to make

Figure 3-1
*The Convincer as
a Sales Letter.*

bicycling more attractive to more people. We feel that our new
shifting system, plus the other improvements and the continuing
high standard of Bellco workmanship, will do just that.

Figure 3-1 *Continued*   We are interested in your ideas. I am attending the
Environmental Improvement Conference in New York next week and
will call you to discuss the new Omnicycle as well as other of
our products designed to improve the environment.

                                        Sincerely,

                                        Flora Gomez,
                                        Marketing Manager

FG/TS
Encl.

passage? There is. It is called the Fog Index and it is the creation of Robert
Gunning.[1]

To see how it works and how you might apply it to your own writing
as well as someone else's, let's take a passage from a government publication and test it for its Fog Index.

> Writing begins in a mystery and ends in a conundrum. At least the
> first half is true, for who can understand the way a word operates?
> Even to phrase the problem is to make it sound like some ancient,
> unanswerable mystery — rather like the questions King Solomon
> asked but never expected to answer. He wondered about the way of
> a man with a maid, but not the way of a word with a man — al-
> though he knew that much study is a weariness to the flesh and he
> knew that of the making of books there is no end. But no doubt he
> would have asked about words if he had thought to do so. And if he
> had lived late enough in history he would have asked what song the
> sirens sang and what name Achilles assumed when he hid himself
> among women, both primarily verbal problems.[2]

To find the Fog Index of this passage, take the following steps:

148   1. Find the average sentence length (words per sentence).
         a. To do this count the number of words in the passage. (Passages
            you select should be no shorter than 100 words. For books or long
            articles, choose two or three selections of approximately 100 words
            each and calculate separately.)

b. Count the number of sentences in the passage. (Each independent   *6*
clause of a compound or complex sentence is equal to one sentence.)

c. Divide the number of sentences (6) into the number of words (148).   *24.7*

Thus the average number of words per sentence for this passage of
writing is 24.7.

2. Find the number of *difficult* words per 100 words. Difficult words are   *8*
those of three syllables or more except for: (a) multisyllabic word
made up of two or more words, such as "however", "moreover",
"notwithstanding"; (b) words that begin with capital letters but do
not start sentences; (c) verbs that have three syllables because of the
addition of endings -ed or -es, such as "consorted" or "confuses."
There are 8 difficult words in the passage of 148 words. To find the
number of difficult words per 100 words, divide the total number of
words, 148, into the number of difficult words, 8, and move the deci-
mal two places to the right.

$$\begin{array}{r} .054 \\ 148\overline{)8.000} \\ \underline{7\ 40} \\ 600 \end{array}$$
   5.4

3. Add the average sentence length (24.7) to the number of difficult
words per 100 (5.4).

   24.7
   + 5.4
   30.1

4. Now multiply the answer to step 3 (30.1) by .4.

   30.1
   X.4
   12.04

The answer is 12.04, or 12. This number represents grade level. Thus, the
passage we just analyzed is written at a twelfth-grade or high school senior
level.

   Evaluate your own writing for readability. If you find that a selected
passage is at grade level 16, how would you go about lowering it? Notice
the style elements that contribute significantly to the difficulty level:

1. Number of words per sentence. Try to keep your average sentence length under 20 words per sentence.

2. Number of difficult words. In our practice passage, for example, what word could the author have used instead of *conundrum?* (Synonyms of conundrum that most people know and use are *riddle* or *puzzle.*)

Chapter 11, which is part of the Troubleshooter's Guide, shows you how to review and revise your writing. It tells you how (1) to adjust information and language to your readers; (2) to keep information simple by summarizing, clarifying, and emphasizing; (3) to use arguments and support for generalizations to make a point clear; and (4) to revise by rearranging, deleting, or recombining to make sentences clear and concise.

If, after completing a memo or report, you are apprehensive about its readability level, apply Chapters 10 and 11 of the Guide. When you are convinced that your writing is clear and concise, check it with the Fog Index. Your intention is not to get the lowest grade level for your writing, but rather to be sure that your readability level is appropriate to your readers.

FORMS AND APPEARANCE OF BUSINESS LETTERS

Our chief concern in this chapter has rightly been with the content of the business letter. But certainly some attention should be paid to the physical representation of the work as well.

The appearance of your letter is intended to make reading the letter easier and more pleasant. You want to draw the reader's attention to what you've written, not to the way you've distributed it on the page. Legibility, consistency, neatness, and an awareness of style are important to the appearance of your letter. You should be consistent, whether you use block, semiblock, indented, or some hybrid form.

Generally, most companies provide style guides which dictate the form and appearance of the correspondence. For this reason, form and appearance are not presented at length in this book, although Appendix A does contain examples and brief discussions of some basic letter forms.

PRACTICAL APPLICATIONS

Exercise 1. Write a Discreet News Release

You have been assigned to Mrs. Johnson's public relations staff (see Figure 2-2). A reporter from United Press International (UPI) wants you to write him a letter describing the new Omnicycle. He wants to use the information in a feature article to be published nation wide. The article will describe the new ten-speed bicycles, but it will be released three months before the new Omnicycles roll off the production lines. While you want Bellco to receive favorable publicity, you do not want to reveal proprietary information on the new bicycles to competitors before the bicycles are on the market. Read the letter on the Omnicycle in this chapter. Carefully select information from that letter which you feel is suitable for a newspaper release. Compose a letter to Mr. John Allen remembering that you will have to clear the letter with Marketing before mailing it.

Exercise 2. Convince Someone to Wait

Read the résumé of Leonard B. Byers, Figure 1-3 in Chapter 1. Mr. Stein, the manager of Industrial Relations and Personnel, has asked you to write a letter to Mr. Byers to tell him that Bellco cannot hire him at this time. The situation is this: he was interviewed twice, by Ms. Gomez, Marketing manager, and Mr. Stein; he passed both interviews, and both persons recommended hiring him for a management position in Marketing. As the offer was being prepared, a freeze was put on hiring at the management level until company overhead rates are determined; you have been told that this will take six weeks. Mr. Stein and Ms. Gomez do not want to lose this applicant; his credentials are excellent. Write him a letter. You can offer him a position, but not for six weeks; but you would like him to be available when the freeze is lifted. Your letter should be a convincer and should be sincere.

NOTE: Be sure to set up your letter by answering the six questions:

1. To whom am I writing?
2. What is my purpose?
3. What is my theme?
4. Should my letter be up-front or a convincer?
5. What are my key points?
6. What action do I want the reader to take?

Exercise 3.   Break the Good News

Read the résumé of Mary Jane Johnson, Figure 1-2 in Chapter 1. You have good news for her; she is to start work in ten days. Write her a letter telling her to report for a personnel orientation meeting that you will conduct on that day at 9 AM. You do not have to mention salary; that has already been negotiated with her. Just tell her she's hired as an administrative assistant to Ms. Gomez in Marketing and that you expect her at the meeting. Remember what your first day on a new job or your first day at a new school was like. In the spirit of good employee relations, try to make her feel welcome at Bellco.

Exercise 4.   Persuade Someone to Pay More

Mr. Roger Brown, President, Save the Environment, Inc. (see this chapter, Figure 3-1), has decided to place an order with Bellco for 20,000 Omnicycles at a price of $75 each. He made his order contingent upon an additional 10 percent discount, which would amount to $150,000. Bellco cannot do this. At $75 each, the bicycles are already discounted 25 percent. The company's margin at this price is only 11.5 percent, which doesn't allow much for contingencies. Mr. Brown is getting a better deal (because of the quantity he ordered and the fact that he is a very good customer) than anyone else.

You are Mr. Belliston's executive assistant and have discussed the problem with him. He has authorized you to write a letter that will convince Mr. Brown to buy the bicycles at the price indicated without the additional 10 percent discount. Review the sample letter of Figure 3-1.

Exercise 5.   Get Tough — Respectfully

The government has not paid its bill, and Ms. Wilson, the controller, is very upset because Bellco's Accounts Receivable are too high. This situation arose when R & D did a study for the Environmental Protection Agency (EPA) under a $50,000 fixed-price contract. The only deliverable item was a final report, due 30 days after the contract was completed. The report was delivered 10 days late because the engineering manager wanted to get some more research results into it. The government contracting officer is delaying payment until he decides if your company can be penalized for late submittal.

You work on the staff of Contract Administration, in Marketing; Bellco's legal advisor told you that there is no penalty clause in the contract and that the government agent is stalling, perhaps because of an internal funding problem. In addition, Mr. Biv told you that the additional research (which caused the delay) was very significant — and was well received by the EPA researchers.

Write a letter to Mr. John Smythe, Contracting Office, Environmental Protection Agency, Washington, D.C. Tell him that Bellco expects full payment on Contract EPA/1745 within 30 days of their receipt of the final report (25 days have already elapsed).

Exercise 6. Slip the Bad News in with the Good

Four months ago, Bellco installed a new Automated Computer Market Checkout System at a Ralph's Market in San Francisco. The system was guaranteed for three months against any defects in workmanship or operation. Mr. James McCleary, manager of the market, called Ms. Gomez yesterday to complain that the system is skipping: it is not checking every item, but skips one item in every ten that pass through. He wants this corrected immediately and, even though the warranty has run out, he does not feel he should have to pay for the repairs. Ms. Gomez has requested you to reply. You check with Service (in Marketing); and they say they can repair it in one day and that a minor modification to the computer is all that is required. It will be one week from today, though, before the repair can be made. You have authorization to assure Mr. McCleary that the repairs will be made at no charge to him. Write the letter. Should it be up-front or a convincer? Write to Mr. James McCleary, Manager, Ralph's Market, San Francisco, Ca. 95741.

References

1. From Robert Gunning, *The Technique of Clear Writing*, rev. ed. (New York: McGraw-Hill Book Co., 1968).

2. Calvin D. Linton, *Effective Revenue Writing*. U.S. Treasury Department Training No. 129. Available from Supt. of Documents, U.S. Government Printing Office, Washington, D.C.

THE MEMORANDUM OR SHORT REPORT ☞

4

The memorandum is the most used (and most abused) document in use today. At Bellco all agreements must be written in memo form. To avoid the creation of a paper mill, Bellco has devised some strict, rather basic approaches to memo writing. All employees are expected to follow them. One key rule is to keep the memo *short*. That means you include only essential information. There is no room in a memo for flowery prose or vague statements. Keep your memos concise, direct, and logical.

ITS CHARACTERISTICS

The memo differs from a business letter in four ways:

1. It is circulated within the company or agency only.
2. It does not have addresses, because it is written on printed forms that have blanks for

```
TO: ————————————————
FROM: ————————————————
SUBJECT: ————————————————
```

(See Chapter 2, Figure 2-1.)

    3. Its SUBJECT heading is equivalent to the title of a report or a headline in a newspaper.

    4. It does *not* have a complimentary closing ("Yours Truly") or a salutation ("Dear Sir").

ITS BASIC PARTS

Every memo, whether it's just three paragraphs or four pages, should have three basic parts. These parts are:

    1. The INTRODUCTION, stating the purpose of the memo and summarizing the most important point.

    2. The DISCUSSION, explaining that most important point or providing supporting evidence or reasons.

    3. The CONCLUSION, telling the reader what to think about, what he has just read, what to do, or what he can expect next.

    It appears from this that our memos are all three paragraphs. No. The introduction could be one sentence:

    I am leaving on the 4:30 flight for Phoenix today.

The discussion could be one sentence:

    In my absence, Frank Williams is in charge of Plant Engineering.

The conclusion could be one sentence:

    Please direct all inquiries to Frank until my return.

    Or, you could write the entire memo in one sentence (but it still contains an introduction, discussion, and conclusion):

While I am away from the plant, Frank Williams is acting manager and will answer your questions until my return.

We at Bellco do insist that you write in complete sentences, and that you pay attention to punctuation and spelling. The Troubleshooter's Guide (Part Two of this book) will help. Chapter 12 is particularly good for specific problems.

ITS REQUIREMENTS

When preparing a memo in this basic format, you should try to meet five requirements:

1. Focus on one main point: know what is the most important message you have to deliver.
2. Adjust to your readers: introduce material and be selective of language and data.
3. Keep it simple: summarize, clarify, and emphasize *the most important points.*
4. Make sense: give support for arguments, assertions, and generalizations.
5. Conclude: emphasize what's important about what you said and what it means.

FIVE TYPICAL SUBJECT AREAS

There are many, many subjects covered in memos. So that we can present some "typical" examples of memos prepared at Bellco, we have categorized these memos under five subject areas. They are:

1. Giving information and direction.
2. Defining a problem.
3. Providing procedures or instructions.
4. Describing a product or service.
5. Justifying your actions.

However, this is *not* an all-inclusive list. It is presented here simply for the convenience of classification. Whatever type of memo you write, be sure it includes the three basic parts and meets the five requirements.

Giving Information and Direction

The memo in Figure 4-1 provides employees with directions on writing memos. It can and should be used as a model for *all* memos written within the company.

Quality Environment Division

DATE 30 September 19__

TO: All Personnel

FROM: A. D. Belliston, President

SUBJECT: Sample Memorandum

Figure 4-1
A Sample Memo-randum.

    This sample memo is in response to your request for a model showing the elements required in this type of document. Note that the three parts of this memo represent the basic structure of typical reports: Introduction, Discussion, and Conclusion.

    The first paragraph you have just read represents an Introduction because it has told you what this memo is about, why it was written, and the main point it will cover. The paragraph you are reading now is a Discussion because it develops the main point stated in the Introduction. It gives examples

and explanations of the parts of this memo. The final
paragraph will conclude with a restatement of the
main point's significance to you, the reader.

The Conclusion helps the reader grasp the most
important point summarized in the Introduction and
clarified in the Discussion. In a memo as brief as
this one, you would not need much restatement -- only
enough to remind readers of what they should be
thinking about, advise them of some action, or let
them know what action they can expect. From this date,
any memo lacking this kind of conclusion will be
returned to its writer for revision.

Defining a Problem

Writing this kind of memo can be difficult. Often the problem is
complex or highly technical. One sentence, one paragraph may not be
enough. The example we will work on here is relatively difficult, yet the
final version of the memo (Figure 4-2) is on one page.

We take you through the steps that the writer followed in preparing
his material on noise pollution. The writer keeps to the Bellco format of
introduction, discussion, conclusion. He also keeps in mind the five requirements of good memos noted earlier. Let's follow through with him.

The Introduction. Introduce by summarizing your most important
point, your purpose in writing, the purpose in doing the work you are
writing about, the background of that work, and the makeup of your
document.

1. Tell your readers what you're writing about.
The memo should describe noise regulations and how Bellco should cope
with them.

2. Tell them why you are writing.

The memo should provide a basis for evaluating those noise abatement measures best suited to the company's needs.

3. Explain why the work is necessary.

Bellco must comply with new standards set by the Noise Control Act of 1976.

4. Describe the background of that work.

The current noise control program is based on standards set in 1964, allowing levels prohibited by the new regulations.

5. Describe the document itself.

The memo should show options available for complying with the new regulations; this memo consists of a brief history of noise control, a summary of current abatement and control measures applied by companies of Bellco's size and circumstances, and some suggestions for further action.

The Discussion. Discuss your subject by making a general statement and supporting it by (1) narrative, (2) enumeration, (3) definition, (4) description, and (5) explanation — singly or in combinations. The writer of the memo on noise pollution, Roy G. Biv, made notes for the memo which were appropriate to each of the five writing styles. He didn't use them all in the finished product (Figure 4-2), but let's look at them in order to see what kind of information is appropriate for each style.

1. Tell the story of what happened.

Noise pollution is a serious problem. The Walsh-Healy Act came about because of estimates that serious damage to the hearing of employees in large plants was becoming more prevalent. In 1974 plants surveyed in five states showed that constant noise exceeded safety limits. In one plant alone, 75 out of 100 employees were found to have impaired hearing after exposure to constant high noise levels.

2. List relevant facts.

Cases of damage to people and property from excessive noise have been compiled in books issued by the World Health Organization, the Public Health Service, the American Industrial Hygiene Association, and the Acoustical Society of America.

3. Define key terms.

You can define by synonym (most common), by example, or by "working definition" (giving a description in terms of what the object does or how it is used).

By synonym: "Noise is unwanted sound."

By example: "Noise in the sky is unlike other noise in that it is not localized. For example, a neighborhood five miles from an airport could hear noise all day long if the wind came in the right (or wrong) direction."

By working definition: "A sonic boom is a shockwave of compressed air created as the airplane pushes the air aside. If a plane is at 70,000 feet, its boom area can extend 80 miles across the earth below."

4. Describe relevant factors.

The basic technique of description is to start by defining key terms, then give a thumbnail sketch or general impression, then list details in a consistent order (outside-to-inside, left-to-right, etc.). Compare these key elements to familiar things, preferably in terms readers can visualize, and explain them:

The basic instrument for measuring sound pressure, a sound level meter, consists of a calibrated microphone, an amplifier, and the indicating meter. The microphone responds to variations in pressure and transduces them into an electrical signal which is electronically magnified. The logarithm of the signal is shown on the meter in decibels. The sound level meter looks like . . .

5. Explain with a typical example or a composite example (made up of several).

Sounds over 85 db heard continuously for long periods threaten hearing. One result can be "boilermaker's disease," so called because earliest sufferers worked in factories where boilers were riveted. Prolonged exposure to sounds over 85 db may result in a temporary adjustment of the ear to the higher level. Thus all sounds heard afterwards will sound fainter than usual. Normal hearing returns after a few hours or a few days. With more exposure, perma-

Composite example

nent damage to the ear is quite possible. When this damage is to the inner ear, it is incurable.

Specific example

Dr. Samuel Rosen's study of native Mabaan Africans in the Sudan showed that their hearing was as good as or better than that of the average North American at the age of 25. The loudest sounds a Mabaan ever hears is the sound of singing or shouting at a tribal dance.

Typical example

John Smith works in a foundry where the noise level is carefully controlled to moderate levels. On weekends he rides his motorcycle or cuts his lawn with a power mower. Because he lives near the airport, he is disturbed by levels of 60 db with windows closed or 70 db if they're open — and 90 db to 100 db if he is outdoors.

The Conclusion. Conclude by concisely reviewing the highlights, reminding the reader of their importance, and recommending what he should do, think about, or expect.

Don't just stop — Conclude! Common sense would tell your reader that if he has any further questions he should contact you. But only you can tell him how, when, and where to do so:

You can reach me at Extension 2468 from 9 A.M. till noon.

Your conclusion should be as factual and informative as any other element of your document.

1. Review the highlights.

Not everything in your document has equal importance. It is up to you now to point out what points were of most importance. In effect, you are *analyzing* your data.

There is strong evidence that high, constant noise levels, when combined with peak momentary levels, contribute to eventual hearing loss.

2. Remind the reader of their importance.

Computers can *accumulate* and *analyze* data, but it takes human intelligence to *interpret or apply* that data imaginatively.

While noise from any one source may be harmless in itself, it may contribute to the cumulative impact on the ear, sometimes around the clock, that prevents the eardrums from relaxing and thus raises the hearing threshold so high as to cause hearing loss.

3. Recommend.

While formal recommendations may not always be in order, you ought, nevertheless, to offer suggestions on what the reader should think about or what he can expect to happen next. Don't just stop.

It is now clear that the new federal standards, as stringent as they are, may not be enough protection, and perhaps what is needed is a federally regulated hearing conservation program.

Quality Environment Division

TO: A. D. Belliston, President

FROM: R. G. Biv, Manager, Research and Development

SUBJECT: Can Industrial Noise Be Controlled?

All firms doing business under the Walsh-Healey Public Contracts Act of 1976 must protect their workers against noise exposure when constant in-plant noise levels exceed 50 db. In addition to these limits, noise levels from impulse - as in explosive air - or from impact - as in drop-hammer operation - must not exceed 140 db at any time. In order to meet these standards, Bellco needs a continuing program of noise abatement and control.

The Engineering Department has already developed

Figure 4-2
Example of a Memo Defining a Problem.

a system of monitoring the factory area with strate-
gically placed sound level meters. The Industrial
Safety Department has begun a regular program of testing workers' hearing periodically. And the Manufacturing Department has redesigned some equipment,
modified noisy machinery with mufflers, and installed
enclosures around certain work places. Such efforts
as these have proven successful, but they have been
random and uncoordinated.

Figure 4-2
Continued

It is therefore proposed that the Company form
a task force charged with developing a coordinated
plan for noise abatement and control that would in-
corporate individual programs in various departments
and include measures for protecting workers in all
departments. Such measures could include: (1) Instal-
ling sound absorbing materials; (2) Using noise specifications when purchasing new equipment; and (3)
Purchasing types of equipment with lowest noise
levels. A task force for this purpose can be formed
now, and at no added costs, from members of the
Industrial Safety Department -- all of whom have
expressed willingness to serve, and now wait for
management approval.

Providing Procedures or Instructions

Bellco, like most large organizations, requires that personnel perform similar tasks in similar ways, for which the guidelines commonly
appear in writing under the heading of "procedures" or "standard operating procedures." Office personnel follow standard procedures or instruc-

tions to ensure consistent practices, and factory personnel follow them to ensure uniform products. In all cases procedures have the effect of "laws," and are thus written as accurately and as clearly as possible. They commonly include three kinds of information:

General Conditions. These procedures or instructions tell who must do what, where, when, and how; what equipment, material, and facilities must be used; what general procedures must be followed; what precautions must be observed.

Special Conditions. These procedures list specific requirements, such as certification or licensing of personnel; use of hygienically clean rooms; or the presence of security people.

Specific Steps. These instructions are commonly written out in this fashion:

1. This procedure describes the assembly of . . .
1.1 Components required are . . .
1.1.1 Parts required are . . .
1.2 Tools required are . . .
1.3 Materials required are . . .
1.4 Company specifications applicable are . . .
1.5 Special precautions required are . . .

2. Before starting assembly, consult TM 47-8, "Soldering Manual."
2.1 Clean all contacts with stiff bristle brush and solvent.
2.1.1 Dry off excess solvent.
2.1.1.1 Air blast.
2.1.1.2 Sponge with clean gauze.
2.2 Mount connector in plug vise.
2.2.1 Ensure that open side of cup is up.
2.2.2 Ensure that cups are at an angle of 45° from perpendicular.

Note that each step, no matter how small, is numbered. Note also that the language *commands* ("consult . . . clean . . . dry"). A quick reading of the memo in Figure 4-3 reinforces our perception of the procedural memo as one that commands precisely.

BC Quality Environment Division

TO: All Personnel
FROM: Catherine Robbins, Publications
SUBJECT: Revised Procedure for Preparing Inter-
           departmental Proposals

Effective immediately, proposals shall be simplified so that they may be read quickly and understood on first reading. For this purpose, they shall
be limited to one page, 8½-by-11 inches, double-
spaced with pica type, and with standard margins as
specified in Office Procedure 741-1911. They shall
follow the format outlined below:

1. The first paragraph shall state (1) the purpose of the memo, (2) the objective of the
   proposed project in terms of (a) the problem,
   (b) the scope of the study, and (3) explanation of unusual terms.

2. The second paragraph shall describe the
   approach proposed: (1) What will be done, (2)
   Why it will be done that way, (3) Where it
   will be done, (4) Who will do it, and (5)
   When it will be done. Budget and schedules
   shall be supplied upon request.

3. The third paragraph shall (1) explain anticipated problems in doing the proposed study,
   and (2) conclude with a summary of (a) antic-

Figure 4-3
Example of a Memo that Provides Procedures or Instructions.

```
ipated results and (b) their application to

the problem described in 1.2.a.
```

```
Failure to follow this procedure will be cause for

rejection of the proposal.
```

Describing a Product or Service
As a rule, describe anything by relating it to something your readers know.

1. Name it.

    "The CPT (*C*urrent *P*rocedural *T*erminology) System . . ."

2. Classify it in familiar terms.

    1. Place it in its general class or family:
       ". . . is a comprehensive book . . ."
    2. Place it in its specific class or family:
       ". . . that lists medical terms and procedures by a five-digit code . . ."
    3. Relate it to familiar items in its class or family:
       "Like a telephone book . . ."

3. Explain what it looks like.

    1. Talk about details in some consistent sequence: clockwise, left-to-right, outside-to-inside, first-to-second, etc.
    2. Use some familiar physical comparison: geometric shapes (square, oval, octagonal, etc.), colors, sounds, touch (smooth, sharp, bristly, etc.).
    3. Provide dimensions.

4. Tell what it does or can be used for.

    "The CPT System simplifies keeping of medical records and provides doctors with quick access to . . ."

5. Explain how it works.

"The System replaces 150,000 different terms, reducing them to 5,000 which are more accurate and readily adaptable to computerized systems."

Figure 4-4 shows us a memo that describes a product. Notice how different this memo is from the sales-oriented business letters on products which we saw in Chapter 3.

Quality Environment Division

TO: Carl Fujii, Manager, Manufacturing

FROM: Shirley Norris, Research and Development

SUBJECT: Prototype FORFEX Cutting Tool

Figure 4-4
Example of a Memo that Describes a Product or Service.

The model shop has delivered the prototype of a new cutting tool, the FORFEX, developed by Andy White's section and now ready for your inspection.

The FORFEX is assembled from four parts cast from low-carbon steel and machined. The cutting edges on one side of each of the two long pieces feature a bonded tungsten alloy ground to a high degree of sharpness.

The two long pieces are held together by a common machine screw. A tension plate of spring steel, mounted between the longer pieces, keeps constant pressure on the cutting edges as they are opened and closed by thumb-and-finger action. Open, they form an "X".

The device cuts paper and similar thin materials
by shearing action. The thumb is placed in the smaller
hole, while the index and middle fingers are placed
in the larger hole. Applying pressure with the thumb
and fingers opens or closes the cutting edges, an
operation easy for children as well as adults and
lending itself easily to use in schools, homes, shops,
and factories, wherever there is a need for simple
cutting.

One weakness of the current design is the sharp
point on the blades, a hazard for children. Another
would appear to be the difficulty for left-handed
people in applying appropriate pressure. Other than
these flaws, the FORFEX seems worth your attention,
and will be sent along at your convenience.

Justifying Your Actions

In a business environment, you are often required to justify some
action you've taken. There is a strong similarity between (1) supporting an
argument, (2) providing a justification, and (3) presenting evidence to lend
credibility to a theory. Remember that any argument must have a *conclusion* and *reasons* for accepting that conclusion.

CONCLUSIONS may be introduced by these words:

allows us to infer that . . .	points to the conclusion that . . .
bears out the point that . . .	proves that . . .
entails . . .	so . . .
from which it follows that . . .	suggests very strongly that . . .
hence . . .	therefore . . .
I conclude that . . .	thus . . .
implies that . . .	we may deduce that . . .
indicates that . . .	we may see that . . .
leads me to believe that . . .	

REASONS may be introduced by these words:

as indicated by . . .	in view of the fact that . . .
as is substantiated by . . .	may be deduced from . . .
as shown by . . .	may be inferred from the fact that . . .
because . . .	on the correct supposition that . . .
for . . .	since . . .
for the reason that . . .	

For an argument, use this sequence: "Because of (reason 1) and because of (reason 2), we may conclude that (conclusion)."

For a "justification" or recommendation: "In view of (factor 1) and in view of (factor 2), we recommend (or request). . . ."

For a theory: "Since this is so and since that is so, it is probable that this is also that."

Figure 4-5 is an example of a memo justifying an employee's actions. As you read through it, make a note of the words that introduce reasons.

Quality Environment Division

TO: Chandra Wilson, Controller

FROM: Robert Walsh, Purchasing

Figure 4-5
*Example of a
Memo Justifying
an Action.*

SUBJECT: Purchase of D-Systems Model 13078 Computer

Just prior to the close of our fiscal year, I purchased D-Systems new Model 13078 computer to replace the Model 130 computer being phased out of their product line.

I purchased the computer at the request of Mr. Biv and with the approval of Ms. Gomez. I am convinced that the Model 13078 is ideally suited to our large-volume, continuous operation. It has the fol-

lowing advantages:

    1. Requires little maintenance and no additional

       training of Bellco personnel.

    2. Uses less power and occupies smaller space

       than the 130.

    3. Represents savings of 50% in operating costs

       over the 130.

In addition, D-Systems reports that the 130 is con-

sidered obsolete and that replacement parts will

become hard to get in the future.

    Since Model 13078 increases our efficiency at

lower operating costs and because R&D and Marketing

both approved its purchase, I bought the computer

using year-end internal research and development

funds.

PRACTICAL APPLICATIONS

Exercise 1. Describe a Product in Memo Form

Mr. Biv has asked you to prepare a memo for Mr. Belliston, describing the company's new product — the Bellcocycle. Prepare the memo from the raw data Mr. Biv has provided below. The subject of your memo is to be an operating manual for the cycle.

    1. Every Bellcocycle has an adequate muffler.

    2. Each rearview mirror reflects the driver's view for at least 200 feet.

    3. The motorcycle model weighs less than 1500 pounds.

    4. Bellcocycles come as motorcycles, tote-goats, trailbikes, and minibikes.

5. A motorcycle is defined as any motor vehicle other than a trac-tor having a seat or saddle for the use of the rider and designed to travel on not more than three wheels in contact with the ground and weighing less than 1500 pounds, except that four wheels may be in contact with the ground when two of the three wheels are a functional part of the sidecar.

6. Seats are adjustable so that any driver can reach the ground with his feet while sitting astride the seat, and so that when he is seated and holding the handlebar grips, his hands are below his shoulder height.

7. A motordriven cycle is any motorcycle, including every motor-scooter with a motor, which produces less than 15 gross brake horsepower. Generally, this means vehicles with an engine size of less than 125 cc.

8. Minibikes and similar vehicles may fall within the definition of either motorcycle or motordriven cycle, depending on brake horsepower; and if such vehicles are operated off the highway, they are classified as off-road vehicles.

9. The Bellcocycle minibike model has an engine of 100 cc.

10. The Bellcocycle trailbike has an engine size of 125 cc. for rough, rugged off-road use — especially in mountains.

11. The minibike model may be licensed for highway use.

12. All Bellcocycle models are designed for use by drivers who are at least 15½.

Mr. Biv needs your memo before the close of business today. Thanks.

Exercise 2. Write a Procedure Memo
TO: The Writing Section
FROM: Catherine Robbins
SUBJECT: Instructions for Changing a Flat Tire on Bellco Vehicles

Please write a procedure memo which will instruct Bellco employees on the proper methods for changing a flat tire on company vehicles. The following information was put together by motor-pool personnel. Use what you feel is essential. Rearrange, add, delete where you think appropriate.

1. Jack up car.
2. Remove wheel and put lugs in hub cap.
3. Put spare tire/wheel on car.

4. Remove jack, lug wrench, hub-cap-removing tool, and spare tire from trunk.
5. Set the brakes.
6. Lower jack.
7. Loosen wheel lugs.
8. If car is on a hill, block the wheels.
9. Replace and tighten lugs.
10. Remove hub cap from wheel.
11. Replace hub cap.
12. Drive to nearest Bellco auto facility and have tire repaired.
13. Remove wheel blocks.
14. Put jack, tools, and flat tire in the trunk.
15. If car cannot be removed from roadway, place flares.

Exercise 3.   (Optional) Prepare a Flowchart Instead of a Procedure Memo

In the procedure memo, Exercise 2, you are trying to explain in chronological order (from the first step to the last) the proper way to change a tire. A very effective technique for giving instructions of this sort is the flowchart. You may have simultaneous and alternative actions to chart. It might start like this:

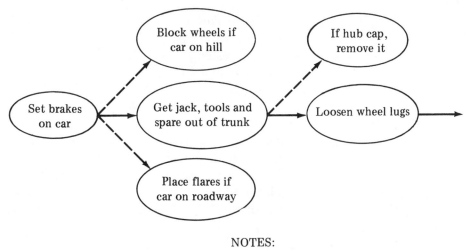

NOTES:
    Unbroken lines indicate required activities.
    Dotted lines indicate possible activities.

Exercise 4. Define a Problem in a Memo
TO: Roy G. Biv, Chief Research
FROM: Carl Fujii, Mgr. Manufacturing
SUBJECT: Bellco Towers Test Data

Test data from the Bellco Towers project accumulated over the past four years remains in raw state because this section suffered a cut in manpower during the last budget slash, and we have no one capable of preparing the report you requested last Tuesday.

I am therefore supplying the raw data rather than the report, hoping that your section will be able to handle it. In fact, I'd appreciate it if you'd have your new employee write this report. I'd like to see the report in its finished form anyway; and this would give me a chance to see a sample of the new writer's work, on a subject I'm quite familiar with. Many thanks.

Please note that some of the data are inappropriate and should not be included in the report.

DATA

1. Bellco Towers has 40 floors.

2. It straddles the Los Angeles Freeway near the Avenue 88 off-ramp.

3. Neighbors call it "Off-Ramp Towers."

4. It has had full occupancy for the past four years.

5. The Research Division requested the Test Section to run a continuous program to monitor environmental effects on tenants.

6. One component of the program tested children's learning ability.

7. We focused on the relationship between noise pollution, hearing, and reading ability.

8. Children from floors 30-40 were average for their social class.

9. Children from floors 1-10 ranked in the 51st percentile.

10. We tested children's ability to discriminate between small, but important distinctions in speech sounds.

11. Some words sound very similar, like *gear* and *beer*, *cope* and *coke*, *guile* and *while*.

12. Noise levels were:

floors 1-10, 66 db
11-20, 63 db

21-30, 60 db

31-40, 57 db.

13. Average reading rank for tenants' children's social class would be in the 85th percentile nationally, meaning only 15 percent of all children in the U.S. read better.

14. We tested the number of word pairs heard correctly.

15. Children on floors 11-20 were in the 63rd percentile.

16. Children on floors 21-30 were in the 67th percentile.

17. Children on floors 31-40 heard an average of 25.8 word pairs correctly.

18. Thirty word pairs were tried on each group of children.

19. Children on floors 1-10 heard an average of 22 words correctly; those on 11-20, 23; and those on 21-30, 25.

20. It is well known that a subtle loss in discrimination between speech sounds can adversely affect a child's ability to read.

21. The social class of the tenants of Bellco Towers is assessed to be quite uniformly the upper-middle class.

Exercise 5. Prepare a Memo Justifying a Pay Raise

Your supervisor, William Gabriel, has notified you that he failed to obtain a better-than-average (3%) merit increase for you. You were certain that you would receive a 6% raise, and you tell him of your disappointment. He tells you that a three-man committee must review and approve all larger-than-average raises, and he was unable to convince them to approve yours at 6%. However, he promises that he will take your case to the committee again, but only if you write a memorandum clearly stating your position. The committee meets today and not again for two weeks. You have one hour to prepare your case.

You hurriedly jot down some "reasons" which you think support your case, such as you:

1. were not absent or tardy during the past year.

2. voluntarily worked overtime without pay on some important new business projects.

3. were always punctual at meetings and in meeting deadlines.

4. had little or no controversy or disagreement with your supervisor.

5. were careful not to add to the "grapevine" or to engage needlessly in gossip during work hours.

6. conceived an accounting form which is now being used by the company and has resulted in savings of hundreds of dollars per month.

7. were selected to serve as a member of the company Credit Union.

8. filled in for your supervisor who was on special assignment, and successfully conducted two negotiations with important customers.

9. established a "letter routing system" which has been effective in keeping "urgent" correspondence from ending up in the dead-letter file as had happened frequently in the past.

10. have been loyal to the company and have participated in bond drives, the company picnic, and the Christmas party.

Select the appropriate reasons from the list of ten, and prepare a memorandum that will convince the committee to give you a 6% raise. You will probably want to rephrase and reorder the points selected.

Exercise 6. Write a Trip Memo

A trip memo (a short report) is often a brief factual account of your meetings and events on a business trip. It is the kind of memo that provides information and direction. The information you provide should be of importance to the company and its business posture. You should prepare a distribution list which includes all personnel of the company who have an interest or need-to-know.

Often, a trip report must be persuasive, too. For instance, in the following assignment, you, as a member of Marketing, know that if the company does not take proper action on your information, a very important profit-making program will be lost to a competitor.

Before writing, consult the memo-writing guidelines in Chapter 4. Also consult the Bellco organization chart, (Figure 2–2), and the biographical sketches of Bellco personnel, in the section entitled "Who Is Bellco?" (both are in Chapter 2).

On the basis of the following information, write a trip report to Ms. Flora Gomez:

1. As a member of Marketing, you were sent on a trip to visit Bellco's best customer, the U.S. Army Electronics Command, Fort Monmouth, New Jersey.

2. The base is located near Asbury Park, a seaside resort.

3. The Army has been buying amplifiers from Bellco.
4. Electro-Technology, a competitor of Bellco, makes amplifiers too.
5. On the third day of your visit, Mr. Byall, the Army purchasing agent, said that he's preparing a new, competitive amplifier procurement in the fall of 1977.
6. It is now June 1977.
7. Mr. Sparks, the Army chief engineer, told you that they just tested the newly developed Electro-Technology amplifier and it registered a noise figure of 5 db.
8. Bellco's Parametric Amplifier unit is 6 db.
9. The price of the Electro-Technology unit is the same as ours.
10. You remember someone in R & D at Bellco saying that we could build an amplifier at 4 db if we only had $50,000, three months, and three key engineers.
11. Len Romano told you (off the record) that the three key engineers are already assigned to other important contracts at Bellco.
12. You went to lunch at the Seaside, a resort hotel and restaurant in Manasquan and had prawns.
13. Profit on Bellco's amplifiers is 25 percent per unit, and we sold 4,000 to the Army last year.

Exercise 7. Write a Combination Memo — Providing Information and Defining a Problem

Write a memo reply to the trip report which is based on the following information.

You work for the Chief Engineer, and you are particularly upset with Marketing because of the recent memo on the Parametric Amplifier. This memo was critical of Engineering. While you are conscious of the need for company unity (stressed by President Belliston), you also feel the need to defend your position and your department.

You have the following information to work with:

1. You talked to Marketing over a year ago about developing a mixer diode (MD). The MD does the same thing as the parametric amplifier (PA), but at the lower noise figure of 4 db.

Marketing turned down your request for funds to start development at that time.

2. You have personnel available to work on the mixer diode development in time to meet the Army's needs, and you do not see a conflict with any ongoing programs. (You suspect that Marketing is not happy with the technical caliber of the people available; you are satisfied with their competence.)

3. You need more technical information on the Army's requirements. You had suggested that a systems engineer accompany the salesman to Fort Monmouth, N.J., but you were turned down.

4. You suspect Marketing of "engineering" the new PA/MD in advance.

5. You were not consulted regarding the $50,000 estimate, and you disagree with the dollars and the manpower requirements as proposed by Marketing. Your own engineering estimates, based on a careful requirements study of manpower, materials, and laboratory equipment, is 100,000 dollars and five full-time engineers for four months.

6. You want engineers to accompany salesmen on all technical sales trips.

7. Marketing control of proposal funds and Research and Development funds makes it difficult for you to anticipate new business requirements and to staff appropriately to continue necessary R & D.

8. You feel strongly that R & D should have a greater responsibility in sales-related areas — including new product development, customer and market development, and preproposal, proposal, and followup activities.

9. You would like to see a company directive giving R & D more responsibility and flexibility in these areas.

You have the full agreement and cooperation of R. G. Biv. Write a memo to James Burke stating your position. Send copies to the managers of Marketing and of Industrial Relations and Personnel, and to the vice-president of Finance.

Note that two types of information are provided: (1) dealing with the immediate problem as reported in the trip report; and (2) dealing with a longer range problem of company policy and communication.

Exercise 8.   Prepare a Product Description
Write brief product descriptions of one of the following products:

wall-mounted pencil sharpener
mechanical (with rotating handle) can opener, or
hand-held stapler

Write one memo to the staff management and another — on the same subject — to the technicians. Adjust your information and language to your readers. (You will find the material in Chapter 9 particularly useful in helping you reach the right level.)

THE FORMAL REPORT ☞
5

R eports are often looked upon as necessary evils. Yet effective reports are essential to the smooth operation of a business or institution. Often they are overdone: they become merely justifications, defenses, documents to satisfy bosses' whims. Reports such as these are a waste of time, money, and energy.

There are valid reasons for preparing reports. Underlying all of the valid reasons is the basic *raison d'être* of a report: to inform. To do this effectively, a report should be purposeful, direct, objective (as much as possible), and logically developed. Reports range from the informal memorandum to the formal multivolumed research investigation. In between, there are reports that cover many business areas (see Figure 5–1).

There is much overlap among these areas. For instance a report entitled "Bellco's Competitive Position in the Component Market" would be of interest to Management, Marketing, Engineering, and others. So how do you categorize a report? By the addressee or addressees. If the report is being written exclusively for Management, it is classified as a management report. If it has multiple destinations (as most reports do), then as the writer, you should know who on your distribution list is required to

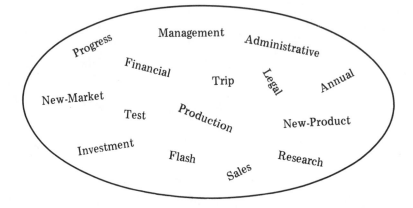

Figure 5-1
*Some of the
Business Areas
Covered in Re-
ports.*

take action. Thus, if you need money to continue a project, your report may be addressed to the controller with copies to other divisions of the company, perhaps including Engineering. If you write the report in engineering terms, you may receive accolades from the engineers; but if the controller cannot understand what you've accomplished, you may not receive any more funding to continue the project.

The only reason you would want to classify your report is to allow you to structure the report for your readers. (Paragraphs 9.17 to 9.24 and Tables 9-2 and 9-3 in the Troubleshooter's Guide show you how to select information for the reader.) Where there is multiple distribution among various levels of the company, you would want to aim the report at the primary addressee, who should also be the one required to take action. In the case of the financial report, that person would most likely be the controller. Does this mean that in explaining an engineering accomplishment to nontechnical personnel, you must write down to the engineers? No. You can provide the controller with the information he needs in sections of the report such as the introduction, summary, and conclusion, and you can satisfy the engineers' need for detail and supporting information in the discussion section. This means, though, that you must provide enough information in the introductory sections and the conclusion to allow the controller to respond favorably to your report.

PLANNING THE REPORT

One of the main differences between a report and a memorandum or note is that a report requires more planning. A memo can often be written after just a few seconds of thought and preparation. For most reports, this is not so. Since clarity and logical development are key ingredients to effective reports, equal weight should be given to the planning or the prewriting of the report as to the writing. This is also true of the oral report. The planning or prepresentation phases are as important to the overall success of the presentation as the delivery of the material.

The prewriting and prepresentation phases are very similar and are described as follows:

1. Establish your purpose.
2. Consider your reader/audience.
3. Arrange your data.
4. Outline your report/presentation.

Key parts of the writing phases are covered in the Troubleshooter's Guide as follows:

1. Write the first rough draft (Chapter 10).
2. Review and revise the draft (Chapter 11).
3. Secure approvals.
4. Publish and distribute the final document.

The presentation phase of an oral report consists of the following steps:

1. Write out the entire presentation and prepare separate note cards from which to speak.
2. Prepare the supporting graphics (rough draft).
3. Dry-run the presentation.
4. Review and revise the presentation and prepare final graphics.
5. Present a final dry run.
6. Give the presentation.
7. Prepare a handout (optional).

THE PREPARATIONS

Why are you writing the report? Why are you giving the presentation? Answer these questions specifically and you have declared the purpose.

Establish Your Purpose

Keep the purpose in front of you throughout the preparation. It does not go into the report but provides the beacon to keep you on track. How do you phrase the purpose? Well, one way might be: "I am preparing this report to inform the marketing manager of the sales potential of the XDR-1400 radar system when used as part of a pollution surveillance system. The market surveyed is Western Europe; the period is 1977–1985; the report is due on 27 February." You have answered the following questions in your purpose statement:

To whom are you writing?	— marketing manager
Why are you writing?	— to inform him
What will you cover?	— market survey — product and marketplace
What period do you cover?	— 1977–1985
When is it due?	— February 27
By what means (how) will you do it?	— formal report
What area (place) does the report cover?	— Western Europe

If your report is required under a contract clause, your purpose statement might read: "This report is submitted for the U.S. Air Force under contract AF 7–4692. It covers the testing of six 35G mixers conducted during February and March. It will inform the AF of the successful conduct of the tests and present a plan for the next phase of the project. The report is due on April 30."

Consider Your Reader

Who, specifically, is your reader? Your audience? Do you know him or her or them by name? Write their names down. As we saw in Chapter 3 on letter writing, and in Chapter 9 of the Guide, it is always to your advantage to know your reader as well as you can and adapt the report to his requirements. What are the questions *the reader* would like answered by your report? In the case of the marketing report, your reader, the marketing manager, would certainly want to know potential sales, potential profit, return on investment, competitive position, potential growth, etc.

If you can list many of the questions your reader or audience might ask, you can preempt the questions by providing the answers as a part of your report or presentation. Again, you are not going to include this material verbatim in your report; you are going to select essential information to be carefully inserted in your outline and then in your report.

Arrange Your Data

Your data can come from internal or external sources. Some internal sources might be personal experience and direct observation — planning, analyzing, evaluating, sampling, interviewing, test data, laboratory data, experimental data. External sources are those that you do not develop yourself. Even though you may have had nothing to do with developing the information and little to do with preparing the original material, since it is going into your report, you are responsible for as much verification as possible and the arrangement of the information so that it becomes an integral part of the report.

At this point in the prewriting or prepresentation phase, you are working with rather large blocks of information. You have some information from Quality Assurance; you have some early test data; you have the laboratory procedures; you have the financial status of the contract. Survey the information you have; question whether each major section is complete, and make some *preliminary* decisions as to approximately where the material might go in the report. Certainly before presenting the actual test data, you would want to state the purpose of the test and the anticipated results, and to describe the test setup and procedures.

Outline Your Report. Apply Chapter 9 of the Troubleshooter's Guide: it discusses approaches to outlining that are effective yet not too time consuming. Remember that your first outline is a preliminary one and subject to change. Group items together that logically go together and be sure you provide adequate support for your main points throughout the report.

As you are outlining, be aware of the illustrations and tables you will need to clarify and emphasize essential data. You should begin preparation of rough draft graphic material; and orders for photographs and for special artwork should be placed early. The same is true for an oral presentation. Decide as early as possible what graphic aids you will need and go about acquiring them. The presenter has the additional problem of deciding what audiovisual techniques he or she will use — that is, charts, slides, film, cassettes, etc.

THE WRITTEN REPORT

The report differs from the proposal in that the author is not overtly trying to sell a product or a service. The term "overtly" is used because often in a report the author is recommending additional work or new work to follow that which has just been completed. Thus, there is a certain amount of persuasion (selling), but it should be based on the merit of the findings rather than on a carefully planned marketing campaign. If the report does not present the findings clearly, objectively, and interestingly, it may fail to convince the reader that additional work is necessary.

Purpose of the Major Divisions

As in proposals, reports can be divided into three major sections: Introductory Material; Discussion; and Conclusions and Recommendations. A well-written report follows a modular concept. It is both inductive and deductive. It is inductive in that it is carefully constructed to guide the reader to draw the same conclusions (before he actually reaches the conclusion section) that the writer has already drawn. The writer must build his report logically so that the reader draws inferences as he reads and these inferences culminate in the acceptance of the writer's conclusions and, consequently, his recommendations.

The report is deductive, too. It provides essential and generalized information early, in sections such as the introduction, abstract, and summary. Since these sections come before the main body of the report and are written for management personnel and casual readers, they must provide enough essential information to allow the reader to grasp the significance of the entire report. Often, conclusions become part of the summary. Supporting information then follows and provides the necessary details.

The modular concept functions for *all* reports. The modular concept simply means that sections of the report are prepared as separate modules so that different levels of readership can then focus on particular parts of the report of interest to them. Figure 5-2 shows the modular concept applied to a technical report.

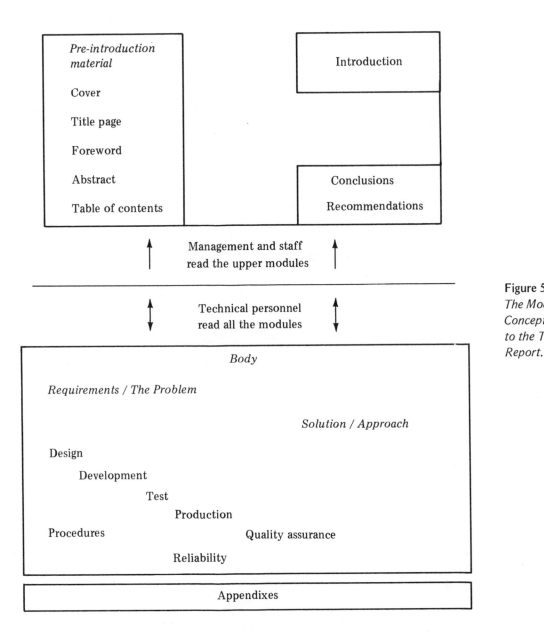

Figure 5-2
The Modular Concept Applied to the Technical Report.

Making the Report Easier to Follow. Data in reports can become very involved and complicated. To make it easy for readers to understand the data and to see relationships clearly among the data, the author should provide tables and figures. Tables are used to show exact data in a form

Center Frequency† (Wavelength)	1.42 GH$_z$* (21 cm)	4.99 GH$_z$* (6 cm)	13.4 GH$_z$* (2.2 cm)	37 GH$_z$* (0.8 cm)
Bandwidth (MH$_z$)	28.4	6	300	300
Sensitivity (°K/sec)	1.1	1.8	0.8	0.8
Antenna Width (°)	20	8	8	8
Accuracy (°K)	±3	±3	±2	±2

*These are called column heads. All material in one vertical band makes up a column.
†The left column of a table is called the stub. It contains titles (or heads) for the rows, which are the horizontal bands.

which allows the reader to compare or contrast the figures readily. An example is shown in Table 5-1.

In a figure, data are shown on a matrix designed to demonstrate the relationships of the information. Presenting the exact information may not be as important as showing relationships; if this is the case, use a figure that shows the material in a graph, as in Figure 5-3.

Tables and figures are not used exclusively to show technical or

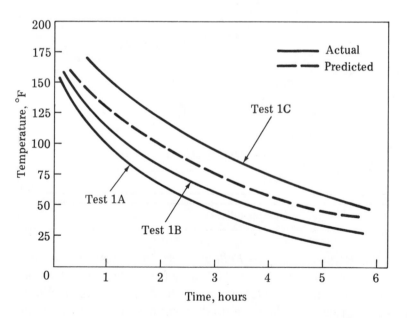

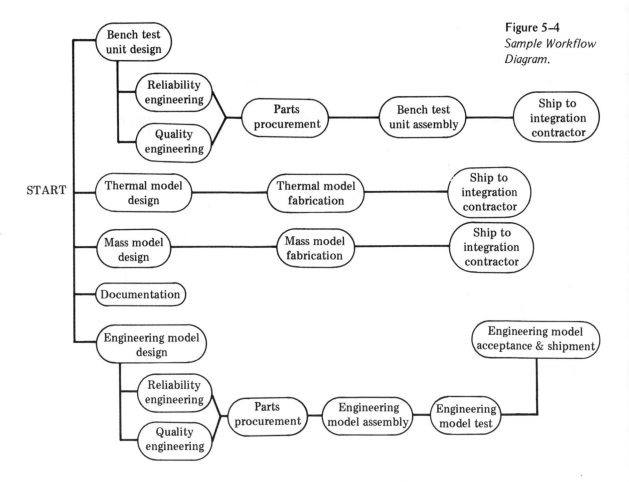

Figure 5–4
*Sample Workflow
Diagram.*

numerical data. They can also be used to clarify concepts, show progress on a contract, demonstrate how the flow of work is expected to proceed, or illustrate a schedule with outstanding mileposts. Figure 5–4 is a sample workflow diagram. Each step is charted in a process — from initial design of models of a new product to delivery. If appropriate, time could be shown along the abscissa (horizontal axis) of the chart. Readers could then at a glance determine when mass model fabrication will be complete, or when the engineering test model will be delivered. A sample program schedule is presented in Figure 5–5. In this figure, readers can see that program management and project engineering start in the first month and continue throughout the 18-month program. They can tell that five quarterly re-

Item	Months																	
	1	2	3	4	5	6	7	8	9	10	11	12	13	14	15	16	17	18
Program management	△																	△
Project engineering	△																	△
Documentation																		
Monthly reports	△																	△
Quarterly reports			△			△			△			△			△			
Final report																		△
Design and analysis	△								△									
Development						△						△						
Engineering model fabrication									△						△			
Testing															△	△		
Delivery																		△

Figure 5-5
*A Sample Pro-
gram Schedule.*

ports and one final report are due, and that the fabrication of the engineering model will take seven months.

Tables, figures, charts, and photographs should be designed to do one
thing — provide clarity!

THE ORAL REPORT

Suppose that the time is approaching for you to present an oral report to
management. You know your purpose and your audience; you have ar-

ranged your information, constructed an outline, and decided to use 20 × 30-inch charts. What do you do now?

1. *Write out the entire presentation.* From all the data you've accumulated and from your outline, write out in rough draft your entire presentation. At this stage, include everything, even doubtful information. It's easier to cut back than to add later. After you have done this, prepare separate note cards from the information. What material do you include on the note cards? Some experienced speakers need only key words or key phrases. Then, by merely glancing at the word, the speaker can launch into another section of his presentation. Others need longer lead-ins to major ideas: they write out sentences or even short paragraphs. Whatever your preference, use the cards only as cues; do not read from them.

2. *Prepare the supporting graphics.* Consider carefully which medium you will use to emphasize key points in your presentation — film, cassettes, slides, vugraphs, charts, or a combination. Each has advantages and disadvantages. Table 5–2 may help you in choosing the right one for your presentation.

When we consider all the material in Table 5–2, we are likely to decide that charts are superior to the other media. But other factors might

Medium	Material Can Be Animated	Lighting Requirement in Room	Speaker–Audience Eye Contact	Audience Participation	Speaker Flexibility
Film	yes	dark	none	none	none
Filmstrip/Cassettes	some	dim	minimum	some	none
Slides	some	dark	none	some	none
Vugraphs	some	dim	minimum	some	some
Charts	some	bright	maximum	maximum	yes

Table 5–2
Factors that Influence Choice of Visual/Audio Aids

mitigate against charts — such as (1) a need for animation to emphasize a point (film would be required for this); (2) a wish to share with the audience the visual impact of the subject (this calls for photographs, sketches, scenes, or assembled data, all of which can be reproduced in vugraphs and slides); (3) a large audience (150 or more participants can see slides more easily than charts). In addition, a mixture of media is acceptable. A short filmstrip could be inserted during a chart talk to illustrate a point. It would also serve to provide a break, a change of pace for the audience.

For management presentations, charts or vugraphs seem to be the most popular. The rules of thumb for both are:

1. Include *only essential* information — what you want the audience to remember.

2. Keep them simple — use color, cartoons, arrows, diagrams or other animation techniques but keep each chart focused on *one* point.

3. Write in individual words or phrases — be terse; no more than 25 words per chart.

4. Make the writing large enough to be visible to anyone in any area of the room.

As the presenter you should:

1. Read the entire chart to the audience first.

2. *Never* turn your back on the audience or any section of the audience. Do not speak to the chart.

3. When showing vugraphs, try to place the screen and projector in positions which do not place you in front of, or in the middle of, the audience.

4. Introduce the material on the chart before showing it.

5. Cover the chart immediately upon finishing with it.

6. Do not dwell on a chart for more than 2 or 3 minutes.

3. *Dry-run the presentation.* If you're fortunate, there will be some people in the organization you can rely on to be objective, honest, and constructive when you run through a practice presentation. If you have the time and the equipment available, have a video tape set up to record the presentation. Then, run it back immediately after the dry run to see first-hand your strengths and weaknesses.

In presenting a dry run, you should advise your audience to allow you to give the entire presentation first. They should take notes as you speak but not interrupt. Then, a general discussion on the overall effect of the talk — strengths and weaknesses should ensue. Following this discussion, a second dry run should be conducted; this time comments should be made at the time someone feels it is appropriate to do so. Dry runs are not a time for defensiveness or ultrasensitivity; neither are they a time for personal attacks. They require an atmosphere of openness which encourages constructive criticism.

4. *Rewrite and revise the presentation and prepare final graphics.* Now you have the comments from your colleagues and a better idea of what the presentation sounds like; revise it to accommodate those changes you feel are appropriate. The presentation may require a major reworking of the organization and development, or it may just need some minor modifications to the diction. Whichever is required, Chapter 11 of the Guide will help you through the review and revision phase.

Since time is a factor in most presentations, it is necessary to decide as early as possible on the graphics you will use. There is always a lead time required in preparing these, whether they be charts or slides. Make the changes agreed to during the dry run and send off the graphics to be completed in final form.

5. *Give a final dry run.* This is always a good idea, even if the original presentation required only minor modifications. Of course, lack of time may make a final dry run impossible. If necessary, give a final dry run, aloud, to yourself or to just one or two of your associates. This will allow you to fine-tune the talk.

6. *Give the presentation.* Be natural! Approach your audience on a one-to-one basis. The best way to do this is to look into the eyes of one person at a time. As you are looking at one person, you are talking to that one person. When speaking to a large audience, you cannot look into each person's eyes; however, you can scan the audience and pick out responsive listeners in each section of the room. In this way, you are speaking to the entire audience while at the same time conversing with individuals in the group.

Another aspect of naturalness is that your movements, gestures, and voice modulation should also be your ordinary ones. You want the audience to pay attention to what you say, not how you say it. Move about easily, naturally. Do not pace, march, or stalk. Gesturing is fine if not done for the sake of showmanship. Of course your voice must be strong enough (if no amplification is available) to reach the persons in the rear row. However, it should be modulated naturally so that neither a low monotone nor a barker's pitch is maintained throughout.

Other key points on keeping natural:

1. Pace your talk. Provide pauses after important statements.

2. Know your introduction and your concluding remarks. If necessary, memorize them.

3. Speak with confidence, not arrogance.

4. Be enthusiastic.

5. Don't be afraid of being imaginative and original. New ideas in both delivery and content will help maintain interest in your talk. For instance, try emphasizing a point by speaking more softly rather than by raising your voice.

6. Avoid clichés. Don't say — "Unaccustomed as I am to speaking," etc.

7. Finish strongly and positively. Leave no doubt that your talk is over.

8. Allow time for, and ask for, questions. Remain standing in front of the group until all questions are answered and you are indeed finished.

7. *Prepare a handout.* It is always good policy to leave some written document in the hands of the attendees. One good ploy is to have copies of the charts reduced to 8½ × 11 inches and stapled together to make a booklet you can give to each member of the audience. Tell them in advance that you have the material for them but give them the documents after you have completed your talk. If you have an associate with you, have him distribute the booklets while you begin to answer questions. They can serve as catalysts for additional questions.

PRACTICAL APPLICATIONS

Exercise 1. Prepare a Formal Report
Follow the suggestions in this chapter, as well as the outline suggested below.

STEP 1 — Selecting the Topic and Planning the Report (complete in 1-2 weeks)

1. Select the subject and determine the basic problem to be investigated. *Limit* the subject to something that can be handled in 10 pages.
2. Start preliminary research by doing the informal investigation. Read about the subject, talk about it, ask preliminary questions.
3. Make a clear, definitive statement of the problem.
4. Break the problem down into constituent parts.
5. Write "Program Plan Proposal" (1 page):
   a. Statement of the problem
   b. Procedure to be followed
   c. Anticipated results
   This will help you develop your preliminary outline.
6. Submit the program plan proposal to your instructor.

STEP 2 — Research (complete in 1-2 more weeks)

1. Begin in-depth research.
   a. Secondary — library
      bibliography cards, 3 × 5"
      note cards, 4 × 6"
   b. Primary
      observation
      interrogation
   Be sure to record *all* information on note cards and label cards by Preliminary Outline topic headings.
2. Update, revise, and rewrite preliminary outline.
3. Hand in bibliography, note cards, and outline to instructor.

STEP 3 — Writing the Report (complete in 1-3 weeks; total from starting date should not exceed 5 weeks)

1. Prepare the rough draft. Concentrate on getting material down on paper. Follow your outline, revising as necessary.
2. Select and prepare illustrations. May include half-tones, line drawings, graphs, curves, charts, and tables.
3. Revise rough draft (as many times as necessary) to remove errors in content and to correct errors in mechanics.
4. Write sections: summary, table of contents, letter of transmittal. (If the formal report is being prepared for readers within your

company, the letter of transmittal may take the form of a memo.) Prepare final version of paper; proofread carefully.

5. Submit report to instructor.

Bellco Formal Report Structure*

Cover
Title page
Letter of transmittal
Table of contents
List of illustrations (optional)
Summary
Introduction
Body of the report
Conclusions and recommendations
Appendix (optional)

*See Appendixes C and D for standard formats of any of these elements.

THE PROPOSAL IN LETTER OR MEMO FORM ☞

6

The proposal is a sales document. To be effective in bringing in new business, it must be addressed to the customer's needs, it must be written clearly and convincingly, and it must give the *reasons* why your company should win the job — technical, management, and price reasons.

A proposal can be written on the back of an envelope, as a business letter or memo, or it can be a multivolume document of several thousand pages. It can be done in one day or take months, sometimes years. It can be submitted to one person or a government agency or private company. It can be for a job worth less than a hundred dollars or one worth millions, even billions. In any event, it must answer the customer's questions and convince him to buy the product or service from you.

Seldom will the proposal alone win a job. It must be part of an overall marketing strategy that includes "preproposal selling." (This could consist of determining the customer's needs — or creating them for him — and then convincing him through contacts and correspondence that you have the solution.) The subsequent proposal gives him the details and provides him with the justification to award you the job.

THE PROPOSAL IS PART OF AN INTEGRATED MARKETING STRATEGY

Often a salesperson will return from a trip flushed with apparent success in his meetings with customers and will say, "Well, I wrapped that job up; it's in the bag. All we've got to do now is submit a piece of paper (proposal) they can use as a basis for a contract." As one who might be called upon to prepare the proposal, you may well react with disbelief. Be skeptical. The same scene may very well be repeated at a dozen competing companies across the U.S. Salespeople are enthusiastic, optimistic, positive. Sometimes just this attitude alone can go a long way toward winning a job if it rubs off on the customer, and he believes the company can do the job. You want that attitude to permeate the marketing department; what you don't want is to have it cause you to underestimate the customer, his needs, the competition, or the job itself.

Last year, a Bellco salesperson went to Alabama to try to convince a government agency to buy a system designed to control the attitude of rockets used in meteorological research. He felt that he had done such a convincing selling job that only a very cursory rewrite of a proposal submitted to another agency a year before would be necessary. He convinced his supervisor and, within a few days, the proposal was submitted. Less than two months later the agency awarded the job to Bellco's competitor in Texas. Why? The customer, in the subsequent debriefing, stated that both systems (Bellco's and its competitor's) would work; that prices were competitive; and that both companies seemed to have adequate personnel. They awarded the job to the Texas company because that company's proposal seemed more specific, gave the evaluators more reason for confidence in the company, provided a strong job-related company-capabilities section, and was interesting. The marketing staff at Bellco knew what the customer needed but ignored it. Their warmed-over proposal saved them money in preparing it but cost them the job.

Think of the fellow who went to a swap meet and bought a dozen shirts at $2 each. He put them in the washer and pulled them out later in tatters. It was little consolation to him that he had spent *only* $24 for a dozen shirts he'd never wear.

The proposal is a key element in the marketing strategy. It should be planned into the strategy to fit with all other sales steps. Thus, during the preproposal phase of the marketing campaign, a salesperson visiting the customer should seek information that can help the proposal writer express ideas acceptable to and of interest to the recipient.

THE PROPOSAL IS A SALES DOCUMENT

The proposal is a sales document. It must sell your product or your service to a potential customer. No matter how complex the subject, the proposal must be written clearly and convincingly. If a contract or purchase order is written, it will be written on the basis of the proposal you submit.

To whom is a proposal written? It is written to a potential customer. It can be the result of a request from that customer, usually in the form of a request for proposal (RFP), or a request for quotation (RFQ). In either case you are submitting a solicited proposal. The customer has written to you, or perhaps contacted your company verbally, and has requested that you submit a proposal to him. You respond to his request by sending him the proposal. The customer can be a single individual, a partnership, a private corporation, or a government agency. You should know your customer well and direct your proposal to his needs.

The proposal may be unsolicited. You may be aware that a potential customer has a need for your product or service but does not intend to request proposals. In this case, you can prepare and submit the proposal to him on an unsolicited basis. There are advantages and disadvantages to unsolicited proposals. The obvious advantage is that if the customer decides to buy, he could very well purchase your product without getting competitive bids. Even if he does decide to write an RFP to get competitive bids, his requirement would most likely be structured around your proposed product or service. The primary disadvantage is that the customer may not be able to get the necessary funds to purchase your product. He may have committed his funds to solicited procurements. You can minimize this risk by conducting a careful preproposal marketing campaign.

If you are bidding on a small construction job (perhaps remodeling a room for an individual), you will find he's going to be interested in how you intend to do it, how much it will cost him, how long it will take you to do it, and how capable you are at the work (as evidenced by your past experience). If he asked you to propose the job in writing, chances are your answers to those four questions would be a satisfactory proposal. On the other hand, a proposal to a government agency can be a very complicated document which may include special contractual commitments, quality assurance plans, cost and program control plans, and facility descriptions.

Regardless of whether you're preparing a short proposal to one person or a large proposal to a government agency, know the customer as well as you can. Include only that information relevant to the requirement. Keep the document appropriate to the customer and his needs. As in all business writing, the reader is the focal point — particularly in the preparation of a proposal.

THE LETTER OR MEMO PROPOSAL

If you have been dealing with a customer for years and he asks you to bid on a particular job, you probably do not have to convince him of your capabilities to do that job. In this case, a letter proposal may suffice. The letter proposal is in the form of a business letter. It should follow the letter format as described in Chapter 3. If it is a bid for some follow-on work to an existing contract (i.e., for an addition to the contract), or if the customer wants some units added onto an existing production contract, write an up-front letter. Early in the letter you would state price, delivery schedule, and any other pertinent information required to allow him to extend and expand your contract.

On the other hand, a convincer may be needed. You may have to persuade the customer that even though the price has increased over his last buy, the product is still a great value and better for him than the competitive product. In preparing the letter proposal, follow the same steps listed for the convincer in Chapter 3.

Letter proposals are very common in business, and chances are that you will be called upon to write one or more during your business career. Often, they follow a phone call in which agreement has already been reached. The letter then serves as confirmation. At Bellco, all letter proposals require an approval signature of an officer of the company.

Letter (or memo) proposals can be written internally, too. A member of the research department might need more funds to continue some research. He or she would write a proposal in memo form to the supervisor (and others who may have an interest), spelling out the requirements and expected achievements. Chances are the researcher would be given one or more opportunities to discuss the project; but discussions won't generate the cash. Very few companies dispense funds unless there is a written request and written authorization to do so.

A HYPOTHETICAL SITUATION REQUIRING A PROPOSAL

The following pages describe a problem. To solve this problem a proposal must be written to secure additional funding. The proposal writer (you) will follow the guidelines suggested in Chapters 8 and 9 of the Troubleshooter's Guide and in the memo-writing procedures discussed in Chapter 4.

The Research Problem

You work in the research department at Bellco. Your project over the last four months has been to develop a Portable Energy Pack, Solar (PEPS). The concept is to build a lightweight, suitcase-size solar energy system which can collect and instantly convert solar energy to power radios, television sets, small appliances, and even help start stalled automobiles. It could be used by campers, recreation vehicle owners, beach goers, — in general, by anyone needing an immediate but relatively low-level source of power. You'll let Marketing worry about the applications and sales.

Your work was going well on the project until the fourth month of the six-month schedule shown in Figure 6-1.

At the start of the fourth month, you were to receive delivery of the solar cells ordered three months earlier. Just prior to the expected delivery date, the solar cell vendor, Cells, Inc., told you they could not meet the delivery date and would be two months late. In a way you were relieved because the design, which you had thought would take only two months, actually took four months. In addition, you want more time to work on the housing itself, but you've run out of money.

You were given $22,000 to cover the entire project: personnel, materials, overhead, everything. The solar cells and other purchases cost

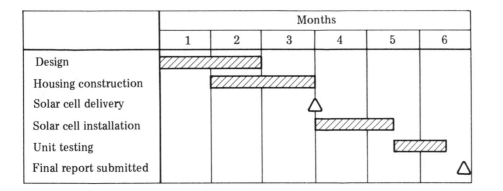

	Months					
	1	2	3	4	5	6
Design						
Housing construction						
Solar cell delivery						
Solar cell installation						
Unit testing						
Final report submitted						

Figure 6-1
The Work Schedule for Development of the PEPS.

you $4,000; and the remaining $18,000 you budgeted at $3,000 per month for six months — to cover your own salary, research assistants, and other laboratory costs. In the first four months you actually spent more money than you budgeted, as shown in Figure 6-2.

As Figure 6-2 shows, you are overexpended by $3,000 in the fourth

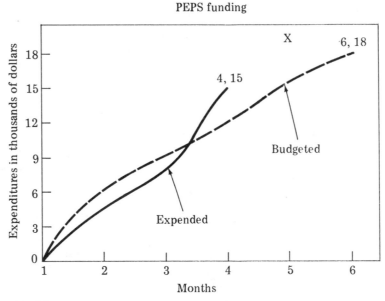

Figure 6-2
The Original Funding for the PEPS Project.

NOTES:
    Budgeted to purchase materials — $4,000
    Expended to purchase materials — $4,000
    X Budget, as expended, runs out 5th project month, April 15.

month. In addition, because of the delay in delivery of cells, you now face a one- or two-month delay. It is time to write a memo proposal requesting more funding and additional time to complete the project.

Constructing the Memo Proposal

As stated before, we are going to follow the Troubleshooter's Guide in constructing the memo proposal. The first thing we'll need to consider is: How do we organize our thoughts? The Guide suggests (paragraphs 8.1 to 8.5) sketching a model of what we want to say; when we do, we come up with something like Figure 6–3. Simplistic? Yes; the secret of organizing thoughts, data, information is to diagram in the most elementary form so that the main point(s) you want to focus on will stand out and be emphasized properly.

So, you need $9,000 more and an additional 4 months to complete the project. You need to do some planning. If you walk into Mr. Biv's office and ask for $9,000 without first giving him a rational explanation for the request, your chances of receiving the funds are slim indeed. You need a convincer. You want to present your case in the most logical and, hopefully, favorable light.

The Troubleshooter's Guide tells us to analyze our assignment and to analyze the requirements of the document (paragraphs 8.15 to 8.17, Figure 8–6, Table 8–1).

Analyzing the Assignment. Let's start with the assignment, the project PEPS.

1. What is the *aim* of the work? It is to develop a small, lightweight, portable solar energy system — one that will save energy, lessen pollution, and be very economical to use.

2. What is the *immediate goal?* To build a research model for testing. If it is successful you will go on to design and build a prototype system.

3. What is the *scope* of the work? Making the working model; this is the whole task right now as far as you are concerned. Your responsibility ends when the model is built, tested, and works. (You may be asked to build the prototype too, but you'll face that issue after the research model is built.)

4. What is the *schedule* for the work? That's the problem area. The schedule was too short and didn't allow contingencies for delays.

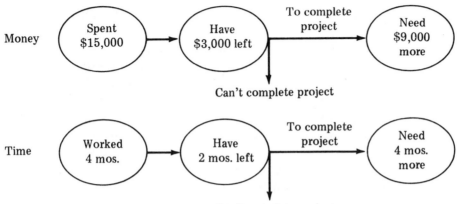

5. What is the *schedule* for writing the memo proposal? Since you
have all the information and are writing the proposal yourself, a schedule
is not needed. It shouldn't take you more than a day. The only thing you
will have to schedule is the typing help.

Analyzing the Requirements of the Proposal. Now let's look at
what is needed in a memo proposal (see the Troubleshooter's Guide, paragraphs 8.17 to 8.18, Table 8-1).

1. Establish the *focal point* of the document: This is easy. The focal
point is the request for more money and time. The focal point is supported by the progress to date and the anticipated results — a working
model.

2. Clarify the *purpose* of the document: In this case, the purpose
and the focal point are the same.

3. Limit the *scope* of the document: What does the reader need to
know? How much detail is necessary to convince him to give you the
funds? In this case, not too much detail would be necessary. You are
making progress and have every reason to believe your model will function
properly in test. You want to convince the reader of this because it is
crucial to your receiving the extension you request.

4. Who will be the *readers?* Let's rephrase that question. Who do we
have to convince to get the funding? The answer in this case is R. G. Biv
who distributes the R & D budget and F. Gomez who, from the marketing
viewpoint, can influence its distribution.

5. How will the document be *used?* This document, an internal

proposal, will be used as a basis for a funding decision. Thus, it must be persuasive.

6. Prepare a *detailed* plan for the document. (Since the internal proposal you are preparing will be brief, you may apply those items of the checklist in paragraph 8.17 of the Guide which are appropriate to a short document. They would include item numbers 1–4 and 7–10. Number 1, collecting information, is completed. So is Number 2: you have selected the memo proposal as your report form. You are ready to prepare your *brief* outline (Number 3) and to write the rough draft (Number 4).

Actually, the sketch you drew earlier serves as your preliminary outline. If you were to put it into a more conventional form (choose one from Chapter 9 of the Guide), the sketch might take a verbal form like this:

Target Statement: To complete the development of PEPS, additional funding of $9,000 and schedule extension of four months are required.

Supporting Points:
1. Research on PEPS to date has been highly successful. No basic engineering problems encountered.
2. Research unit must be built and tested to isolate problem areas with the device and to prove out concept so that prototype can be constructed.
3. Concurrent marketability studies show
    a. There is a *need* for the device.
    b. Bellco is ahead of all competition.
    c. Sales and profit potential are high.
4. Request for funds and need for additional time caused by
    a. Delay in solar cell delivery (vendor fault).
    b. Underestimate of research involved (Bellco fault).
5. Funds needed *now* to keep experienced research team intact, insure continuity of the work, and insure Bellco's competitive lead.

The preceding statement and support constitute your outline. Formal outlines are not required for short reports or proposals. You are now ready to write the rough draft, but before you do, check Chapter 10 of the Guide. It provides some advice for writing rough drafts in the three sections we've been discussing: introduction (beginning), discussion, (middle), and conclusion (ending). Keeping these points in mind, you might make a rough draft of the memo that looks something like the one in Figure 6–4, which was written by an R & D engineer.

The rough draft by Renée Williams is finished. Do you feel the memo is ready to be distributed? Does it follow the Troubleshooter's Guide? Is it convincing? Does it define the problem?

Quality Environment Division

TO: R. G. Biv

FROM: Renee Williams

SUBJECT: Portable Energy Pack, Solar (PEPS) Funding
           and Schedule

Copies To: F. Gomez, L. Romano

The PEPS project is in its fourth month and it appears that all goals established for the system can be reached. The design phase was successful and the construction of the housing is underway. Because the solar-cell vendor did not meet his delivery schedule, we are faced with a need for more funds -- $9,000 -- and an extension of time -- 4 months -- if we are to complete the project successfully.

All evidence in the research to date shows that PEPS can be built successfully and within the specifications agreed to at the start of the project. At the design review meeting in February, all participants

*Figure 6–4
One Version of the Memo Proposal Needed.*

Strong supporting point

Figure 6-4
Continued

agreed that the design of the research unit was

exceptional; the representative from Manufacturing,

Bill Borbuski, said that it was good enough to use

Another
supporting
point

for a production unit. While all project participants

feel confident that the unit, when finished, will

meet all test objectives, we cannot be certain until

the tests are actually conducted.

Marketing research to date has all been positive.

Third
supporting
point

A unit such as this would sell and at a substantial

profit to Bellco, particularly since we can "skim-

the-cream" before other competitive units are out.

When Cells, Inc. told us they couldn't meet the

schedule, I spoke to Charles Paulson, President of

the company. He assured me that we would have deliv-

ery in two months (maximum) and at no extra cost to

Discussion
of problem

us. In addition to this delay, there is a further

delay on the project; we underestimated the design

time (see Figure 6-17); we also underestimated the

expenditures required (see Figure 6-2). We feel

confident now that we are over the most difficult

part of the program, the design, and that the addi-

tional funds and time required now will be offset by

the advantage of having a design which, with only minor

changes, can be used for the prototype unit.

This project is a key one in Bellco's future.

We agreed to put some of our best researchers on it.

If we do not get the additional funding, this team

will be broken up and continuity of research lost.

Both Len Romano, who helped us with the design, and
Flora Gomez feel that Bellco will amortize the entire
PEPS budget, including the $9,000, soon after the
product is marketed.

*Restates
support of
Engineering and
Marketing*

    If we are to maintain the team and continue the
project without additional delays and expenses, your
approval of funds is needed by Friday, April 15. If
approval is not received by that date, the project
will be terminated for lack of funds.

PRACTICAL APPLICATIONS

Exercise 1. Finish the Memo Proposal

This exercise concerns the rough draft memo proposal shown in Figure 6-4. You are being asked to put the memo in final form. Turn to Chapter 11 of the Guide, Reviewing and Revising, which describes the five requirements of a good memo (paragraph 11.3) and gives examples. If you are in doubt about one or more of the requirements, check the appropriate pages in Chapter 11.

1. Focus on one main point.
2. Adjust information and language to your readers.
3. Keep the information simple by summarizing, clarifying, and emphasizing.
4. Make sense with reasons for arguments and support for generalizations.
5. Conclude by reviewing and reminding readers about what to do, think, or expect.

Does the memo need any more revisions? The second half of Chapter 11 in the Guide shows you how to revise by rearranging, deleting, or recombining to make sentences clear and concise. Apply the techniques discussed to this memo proposal and all of your business and practical writing. Rewrite the memo in a final rough draft. (The two charts should be attached to the memo on a separate page. Prepare a third chart which shows how the additional funds and time will be applied.)

Before you type it in final form — and if you have a good, clean rough draft — check it for details. Chapter 12 of the Guide describes some of the more frequent oversights and tells you how to avoid them. It discusses commas, apostrophes, spelling, and typographical errors.

Finish the memo proposal in final form and proofread it. Now, it is ready to be distributed.

The process you followed for the memo proposal is identical to the one you would follow in preparing a letter proposal. You would keep in mind point No. 2 — Adjust to your readers. If the proposal is going to someone not as familiar with your project or request as Mr. Biv would be, then you would have to provide more background and detail to make the proposal complete and convincing.

Exercise 2. Prepare a Memo Proposal

The development section of R & D has successfully tested a new sound suppressor for jet aircraft engines. But they seem to be having trouble getting the company to fund further development. Please write a memo proposal to Mr. Belliston requesting a special outlay of $50,000 to fund a six-month program. This is a panic situation, and it would be appreciated if you write to Mr. Belliston before the close of business today. Organize the data; plan and outline your approach; write the proposal.

Here is the information you have to work with:

1. A jet engine consists of a gas turbine engine producing rocketlike exhaust which propels the aircraft.

2. Conventional mufflers on jet engines cut efficiency by as much as 20 percent.

3. The Bellco muffler cuts intensities for commercial jet planes at a 100-foot range from 140db to 85db.

4. Development section engineers have designed sound suppression systems that funnel the jet stream through 21 small exhaust tubes.

5. The Bellco system sacrifices only 2 percent of the engine's efficiency.

6. Development engineers want to build a prototype system that can be tested to verify theoretical data.

7. They estimate that $50,000 in funding and six months would be required to complete the construction and testing of the prototype.

8. Marketing has committed all its fiscal year research and development funds, but Ms. Gomez approved the sound suppression system program and suggested that a memo proposal be written directly to Mr. Belliston requesting funds from the special, emergency budget.

You represent the development section. When you write the proposal to Mr. Belliston, be sure to include copies to all personnel in the chain of command between the development section and the president. Also include all other personnel who might have an interest.

Exercise 3. Prepare an Individual Proposal

Each member of the class should write a letter or memo proposal on a project of his or her choice. The project should be one in which the student has some special interest or knowledge. Projects could be on subjects such as construction of a garment or construction of a house. The proposal should be addressed to an appropriate member of Bellco management or to a prospective customer and should have the three main divisions: introductory material, discussion (including capabilities), and conclusion. In addition, a one-page cost summary should accompany the proposal. Consult the memo proposal in this chapter for help in preparing the proposal.

The introductory material should include the following:

1. The objective of the proposal.
2. Necessary background information.
3. Description of the general approach to doing the work.

The discussion section should provide the following:

1. What you intend to do.
2. How you intend to do it.
3. Why you intend to do it that way.
4. How long it will take you to complete it.

The capabilities section should convince the reader that you have:

1. The background and knowledge to do the job successfully.
2. The necessary facilities and tools.
3. The time and the help required.

The cost section should include:

1. A cost summary of the hours it will take to complete the job (in $/hour).
2. A list of materials and associated costs.
3. Overhead expenses (including transportation, if applicable).
4. Profit.

The conclusion should sum up your main points by reminding the reader:

1. Of the advantages to him of buying your product.
2. Of why it is important to him.
3. Of what he is to do and when he is to do it.

THE FORMAL PROPOSAL ☞
7

I n the previous chapter, we discovered how to write the short proposal in memo or letter form. Whenever possible, proposals should be kept brief, direct, and to the point. Often, the agency requesting the proposal requires that the proposal be written within a specified number of pages; exceeding this limit would mean disqualification.

A formal proposal is longer than a letter proposal. Generally, it covers a more complex, multifaceted program; and usually it requires more supporting sections to convince the customer. Some sections often included in formal proposals are:

Introduction
Summary
Program Organization
Problem Statement
Proposed Solution
Statement of Work
Company Capabilities
Key Personnel

Facilities
Quality Control
Costs

A formal proposal is usually written by more than one person. Teams are assembled so that individual sections can be written by "experts." In addition, an editing team is assembled to be sure that the document has continuity.

Each proposal is unique — the variables being the job under bid, the customer's requirements and preferences, the time allotted to prepare it, and the proposal format. As we have seen, simple quotations, letter proposals, or multivolume documents can all be done as proposals. The formal proposal, which is the subject of this chapter, is one that presents a solution to a problem and includes, in support of that solution, the management and technical capabilities of the bidding company.

PROPOSAL PREPARATION SCHEDULE

Most companies have committees established to review RFPs (requests for proposals) and to establish proposal teams. The process of response to an RFP may look something like the flowchart in Figure 7-1.

PROPOSAL SECTIONS

Proposal formats vary; however, there are three basic divisions that appear in most proposals: (1) introductory material, (2) discussion of the problem and the proposed solution, and (3) description of capabilities and facilities to perform the job. These three divisions allow the proposal preparer to combine both management and technical information in one volume. It is assumed that a separate cost proposal would accompany it. Thus the entire proposal would consist of two separate volumes.

Introductory Material
The introductory material includes the cover, title page, table of contents, introduction, and summary. Some companies include a letter of

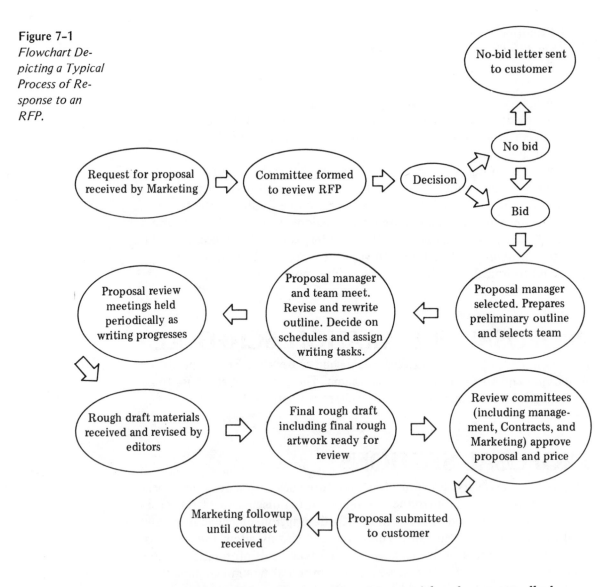

Figure 7–1
Flowchart Depicting a Typical Process of Response to an RFP.

transmittal as part of the introductory material and may actually have a copy of the letter bound into the report between the cover and the title page.

Cover and Title Page. Most companies have a standard format cover and title page. A sample of a Bellco cover is shown in Figure 7–2.

A Proposal For

CLEAN AIR SYSTEMS

September 1978

B2473

Volume I - Technical

Prepared for

The Air Pollution Control District

Los Angeles, California

Quality Environment Division

Copy 3 of 25

Figure 7-2
Example of a Standard Format Cover for a Formal Proposal.

The cover or title page should provide the following information: title of the proposal, company proposal number and/or volume number, date, name and address of agency for whom it was prepared, a customer request for proposal number, and the company identification or logo. In addition, a company proprietary statement may be included on the title page.

Table of Contents. This is a list of the major headings of the material in the proposal. There should be a list of illustrations to identify figures and tables in the report.

Introduction. The introduction is the "selling" springboard for the entire document. Its chief purpose is to show the customer that you understand his problem from his point of view and that you are ready, willing, and able to undertake a program to solve it. The theme developed during preproposal planning should be stated here and developed in depth throughout the document. You also should include general comments about your company's past achievements on similar programs or on programs for the same customer. In general, your introduction should be customer oriented and should be aimed at a top management class of readers. Some of the themes that might be developed here are:

1. You understand his problem from his point of view and how it fits into his current and projected programs.
2. Top management has studied the overall problem and has come up with the proposed solution.
3. You can meet schedule, cost, and performance requirements.
4. You have taken an honest look at your competence for the program.
5. This program ties in with your long-range objectives.
6. This program is related to your experience and current interests.
7. Top management has full organizational control over the program.
8. The full capability of the company will be behind it.

Summary. The summary is included as part of the introductory material because it gives management readers a quick digest of the salient features of the proposal. You are to summarize the highlights of the proposed program, especially with respect to performance, costs (lightly, for these will be detailed in the cost proposal), and schedule goals. Thus, by thumbing through the first few pages, a busy executive can receive a distinct impression of your company's willingness, capability, and approach to solving his problem.

Writing an effective summary takes time. The writer must be aware of the marketing strategy and have a thorough knowledge of the key features of the proposal. In a page or less, the writer intends to convey the essential information in the document. Of course, he undertakes this task only after the document is completed. Since the summary is a very important section of the proposal, the proposal manager and chief editor should collaborate on its preparation.

Often a sale is won or lost by initial impressions. The introductory material makes this impression on the customer. If it is professional, convincing, concise, and correct, it aids your cause significantly. The reader may even look within your proposal for justification to award you the job because of the competence you display in these beginning paragraphs. Help in summarizing information is provided in the Guide, paragraphs 11.11 to 11.18.

The Discussion of the Problem and the Proposed Solution

The very first part of the discussion section should show the customer that you *understand his problem*. The best way to do this is to restate it in your own words. Often you can title the section "Problem Statement" and then go about defining his problem. This is a very good exercise in itself because often a cursory examination of the customer's problem statement does not reveal underlying issues. By stating his problem in your own words you not only show him you know what he needs but you establish communications with him before you launch into your proposed solution.

The discussion section is where responsiveness to the RFP becomes all-important. Basically, the discussion consists of the restatement of the problem, followed by a detailed description and explanation of the Management Plan, the Technical Approach and Plan, and the Development Plan, with pertinent schedules. In other words, it tells what you plan to do — what, why, how, where, and when — what you hope to accomplish, how you are equipped to do the job, and what additionally you will need. Keeping an eye on the theme will help to prevent the discussion from bogging down in details. Some of the kinds of things that might be developed include:

1. You have designed a program management structure specifically for this task.

2. You have the right number and kinds of management people to run it.

3. You have provided for integration of all phases and pieces.

4. You have provided for internal and external communication.

5. The organization charts show how you will operate day by day.

6. The exact role of subcontractors — chosen for their managerial philosophy and talent as well as technical and production skills — is clearly delineated.

7. The availability of key people is stated in manhours (when specified in RFP).

8. You are ready to go. (The program can be readily absorbed.)

9. You specialize in meeting costs and schedules and performance goals.

10. The customer's quality control requirements will be met. (Tell how.)

11. The customer's reliability and maintainability requirements will be met. (Tell how.)

12. The program will be controlled to minimize possibility of cost overruns or schedule delays.

Description of Capability

As with the introduction, there is a tendency for the writer to disregard the significance of the capabilities section: either he treats it lightly, out of false modesty, or he uses "boiler plate" (information that's been used repeatedly and is just dusted off for the current proposal). Yet, as we have seen, it can be disastrous to underestimate your competition. One of the basic objectives of the proposal, therefore, is to demonstrate why you are most deserving of the customer's contract.

It is risky to assume that the customer knows all about you. Even if he has done business with you for forty years, he has new needs now and often new personnel. And for a first-time customer, you may have to dispel a lot of misconceptions about the way you do business or explain capabilities your new client would not have reason to know about. For these reasons, you must take care not to slight the RFP's prescription for related experience.

Even when you do not have directly related experience, you can still define the requirements and show how you have handled requirements on other programs (and what you learned from them). Some kinds of information that might be developed in the capabilities portion, then, would include:

1. You have worked on similar projects; show them graphically (where possible and appropriate).

2. Your biographies emphasize expert and specific experience that is related to the program; eliminate irrelevant details.

3. You have the necessary technical space and facilities for the program.

4. You have special facilities and equipment required for the program (or desirable for it); describe them in detail.

5. You have subcontractors and associates whose capabilities are appropriately described.

6. Your experience in quality control and test programs has been extensive and successful.

7. Your cost estimating is also shown to be reliable.

8. You can draw upon the total capability of the company.

TYPICAL ELEMENTS OF THE PROPOSAL FORMAT— AND WHERE THEY BELONG

Organization Charts (Discussion section)

This portion should include a chart showing how you will organize the team for the proposed task. Include a clear picture of how the project will relate to Manufacturing, Engineering, and other departments in the company, in the customer's agency, and in subcontractors' units. You could start with Figure 2-2 (the organization chart of Bellco's QED) and mark it up to show how the QED would handle the proposed program. Figure 7-3 shows the program reporting directly to the R & D manager and the chief engineer. Lines of authority should be clear at first reading and should include relative positions of managers and of such groups as Purchasing (under Industrial Relations), and Programming and Controls (under Research and Development). This portion often includes discussion of management concepts (e.g., project organization) for the program, along with statements of specific functions and responsibilities. Some customer agencies like to see a list of management requirements on one side of a page and, next to it, some notes on how you plan to meet these requirements.

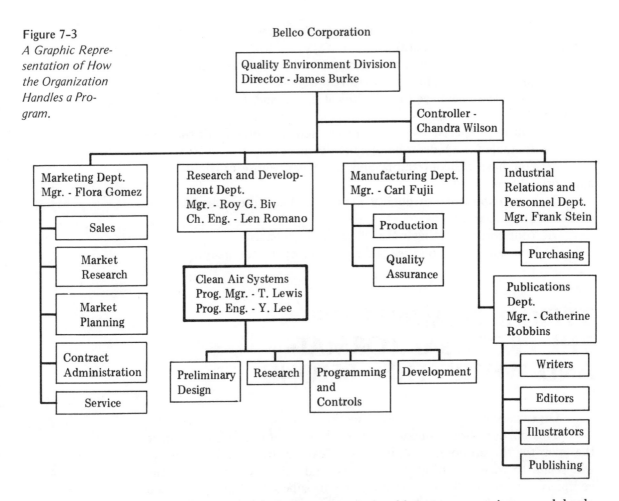

Figure 7–3
A Graphic Representation of How the Organization Handles a Program.

Bellco Corporation

Quality Environment Division
Director - James Burke

Controller -
Chandra Wilson

Marketing Dept.
Mgr. - Flora Gomez

Research and Development Dept.
Mgr. - Roy G. Biv
Ch. Eng. - Len Romano

Manufacturing Dept.
Mgr. - Carl Fujii

Industrial Relations and Personnel Dept.
Mgr. Frank Stein

Sales

Market Research

Market Planning

Contract Administration

Service

Clean Air Systems
Prog. Mgr. - T. Lewis
Prog. Eng. - Y. Lee

Production

Quality Assurance

Purchasing

Publications Dept.
Mgr. - Catherine Robbins

Preliminary Design

Research

Programming and Controls

Development

Writers

Editors

Illustrators

Publishing

Managers assigned to the program should feature experience and background directly related to the proposed program.

Phasing Charts and Schedules (Discussion)

This portion is generally presented graphically, with discussion limited to explaining the charts. The master program plan, or master phasing chart, should include sufficient backup charts to show details of significant areas, or the milestones you hope to attain and when. The milestones must be realistic enough to show honestly where you will be at any time. A sample program schedule was presented in Figure 5-5.

Description of Quality, Reliability, Maintainability, and Cost Controls (Discussion)

These sections require considerable care to demonstrate how Bellco's cost and schedule controls will be tailored to the proposed program. These are the sections in which to lay out the mechanics of the plans in detail, as well as to describe current machinery. Past experience with these controls might also be discussed here unless it is to be discussed under Capabilities. These sections should also explain the philosophy governing the control plans, with the discussion geared to the proposed program.

Evaluation of Manpower Needs (Discussion)

How many Bellco employees will be required to run the program? The availability of Bellco personnel should be explained in terms of: where additional personnel will be obtained; historical accession rate; percentage of previous employees who can be recalled; recruitment and hiring machinery.

Subcontractor Plan (Discussion)

This section could include a statement of Make/Buy intentions — how much of the product Bellco will make and how much it will buy from subcontractors. It often requires a chart showing functional relationships with subcontractors. The object here, as in all the management sections, is to show how the customer's money will be spent. In this section you show him how the money will be spent even when it is "out of the house."

Engineering and Engineering Support (Discussion)

This section, usually the province of Engineering, should feature such design requirements as simplicity, producibility, operability, compatibility of elements, and growth potential.

Manufacturing Plan (Discussion)

This portion is often subdivided functionally:

The Development Plan discusses unique manufacturing processes and techniques which must be refined or developed to meet requirements, along with the plan for putting these into effect.

Tooling should include discussion of the tooling concept for the program. It should cover such features as simplicity and economy of design, interchangeability, quality, and other significant factors pertinent to the customer's problem.

Fabrication should describe methods, processes, equipment, and techniques to be used to fabricate critical parts for the product (e.g., close tolerance, exotic material, unusual size, etc.).

Assembly should describe assembly sequence, handling methods, assembly techniques, and related matters.

Manufacturing Test Plan, although it may be included in the Engineering portion, is sometimes put into the Manufacturing Plan. In either case, it should discuss test levels, methods, equipment, special facilities, and skills for such requirements.

Handling and Outplant Support should discuss the plan for handling, from receipt of raw materials to delivery of finished product. It should explain the kind of manufacturing support required from other organizations outside the division.

Equipment and Facilities Inventories (Discussion or Capabilities)

A facilities plan and list of equipment and space requirements shows the physical means of accomplishing the task. Facilities required should be discussed in terms of how they will also be used on other programs already existing and how they will be phased into the new task. This section should justify new facilities and should include both a timetable for procurement and a statement about how the facilities will be financed.

Related Experience Reports (Capabilities)

This portion is usually compiled from all organizations involved in the proposal and thus should be carefully integrated to avoid repetition or contradiction. Technical ability in related areas should be highlighted to show capability of meeting requirements, quick recovery, adherence to development, and production schedules. Experience in support and maintenance programs should be discussed in terms of such factors as field service, logistics, spares, and operational experience. Experience in quality control and reliability programs, and in test programs, should be emphasized in terms pertinent to the proposal. The discussion of experience (either here or under the relevant section on controls) should be specific about organization, plan, specialized equipment and techniques, sequence, processes, and controls. Reliability of cost estimating is sometimes included here or in the costs section.

Biographies (Discussion or Capabilities)

These should be prepared fresh for each proposal, with emphasis on each individual's experience in the proposed or related field. A suggested format is to include first the man's current status, his immediately prior experience, his background and training, plus any other information (honors, awards, publications, memberships, patents, etc.) related to the program. Generally, the amount of information presented is in proportion to the man's importance to the program. The biographical sketches of Bellco personnel in Chapter 2 could be used as models.

Cost Proposal — Typical Elements*

1. Proposal Cost Summary. This portion, as with the other elements of the costs section, is usually established by the RFP. Often the RFP specifies the use of standard government-issue forms, which are prepared by the U.S. Finance and Contract Administration.

2. Finance. This portion discusses cost reliability; the company's financial structure; prior cost contract experience; a financial statement; and miscellaneous data on burden rates, improvement curves, Make/Buy, facilities charges, royalties, and buy-American certificates.

3. Cost Support Data: Manhours. This portion would include information about engineering development, engineering design, manufacturing development, manufacturing design, tool design and coordination, tool fabrication, quality control, fabrication and assembly labor, and a manufacturing estimate of overtime labor for fabrication and assembly.

---

*The cost proposal is often a separate volume and is submitted as such. This allows the evaluating team to decide on the technical/management proposals without being influenced by money factors. After the technical/management proposals are rated, then the cost proposal is analyzed and factored into the evaluation.

The cost proposal is different from cost controls. The controls discussion just shows the customer that you know (in theory) how to run a program and how to keep costs (not actually stated here) within budget. It describes procedures while the cost proposal discusses actual money.

4. Cost Support Data: Materials. This portion would include data on raw materials, purchased parts, and subcontracts.

5. Cost Support Data: Transportation. This portion would include data on packaging engineering and shipping.

6. Cost Support Data: Administrative. This portion would include data on reports, miscellaneous direct charges, and fee.

ARTWORK AND PRINTING

An important consideration in preparing the proposal document is that its appearance should be as good as its content. Charts and sketches, photos, and the often-neglected covers must be planned as early as possible. The Art Group (illustrators in Catherine Robbins's publications department at Bellco) must know the document's requirements far enough in advance that they will be able to schedule realistically. About two weeks in advance of a firm freeze date on inputs is usually a reasonable amount of time.

It is important that inputs be submitted on a firm schedule and that a freeze date be respected so that there will be no lost time because of revisions in the text. Photos and their captions can be decided early and will require about three days for processing by the Photo Group. Printing or typesetting will require about a week in total, but about three days once all inputs are frozen. It is wise for the proposal manager to order his photos at the outset of the program to enable him to make a selection well in advance of the input freeze date.

Budgets for artwork and printing will vary from proposal to proposal. The best approach is to consult with the Art Group about what kind of document is required and how much can be bought for the money. What the document is to do will dictate what it will be, but short flow times will dictate the quality. Additional costs for overtime can offset compressed schedules only up to a point of practicability. The number of pages, use of color, amount of original art, and method of printing will all influence the cost per document page, which can vary from $10 to $500. (A film in support of the document costs from $300 to $3000.) Budgets can be controlled by adequate lead time, early contact, and early consultation.

HOW THE CUSTOMER EVALUATES THE PROPOSAL

Know how your proposal will be evaluated before you write it. Then prepare it according to this information. The proposal gives the reasons why your company should be awarded the job. The Armed Services Procurement Regulations (ASPR) govern documents prepared for federal agencies. The one dealing with proposals says "reasons should be set forth in such detail as is necessary to justify the award." This "detail" could be merely a price quote or a gargantuan, multivolumed proposal. We have discussed the two-volume proposal; however, the longer proposals may be divided into three volumes: management, technical, and cost. The customer will state whether he prefers a separate cost volume or whether he will allow you to include costs in the management volume.

Why would the customer ask you to prepare two or three separate volumes? When the customer receives your proposal along with those of your competitors, he will probably have two evaluation teams assembled — one consisting of technical experts, the other of personnel versed in program management and cost analysis. Thus, the technical experts can evaluate all technical proposals on their effectiveness to do the job and not be influenced by cost or other factors. After the initial separate evaluations, key members of the two teams are brought together to decide the eventual winner.

Usually a point system is devised to put as much objectivity as possible into the evaluation. For instance, before proposals are received, the evaluation committee, technical and management, may decide that the job is 60 percent technical and 40 percent management. After making this decision, they will meet separately to decide on evaluation criteria. The criteria for the two teams might look like those in Table 7-1.

If four companies were to bid, the evaluation might look something like the display in Table 7-2. Thus, on the basis of this evaluation, Bellco would be awarded the job even though the company did not score as well in management (36 to 38) as did companies A and C. When you know where the evaluation emphasis will be placed, you can direct your proposal efforts to match.

Technical Evaluation Criteria	*No. of points*
Understands the problem	10
Provides adequate solution	25
Technical feasibility	20
Manufacturing	20
Quality assurance	15
Reliability	10
Total Possible	100

Management Criteria	*No. of points*
Management	15
Program plan and schedule	15
Personnel	15
Experience	10
Facilities	15
Subcontracts	5
Price	25
Total Possible	100

Table 7-1
The Point System Assigns Values to the Criteria that Evaluate Technical and Management Factors

	Points					
	Technical	(× 60%)	Manage-ment	(× 40%)	Total Technical and Management	Ranking
Co. A	80	48	95	38	86	2
Bellco	90	54	90	36	90	1
Co. C	50	30	95	38	68	4
Co. D	75	45	85	34	79	3

Table 7-2
Using the Point System to Evaluate the Proposals of Four Companies

WHO PREPARES THE FORMAL PROPOSAL?

As we have seen, a formal proposal is seldom written by one person. Most often it is prepared by a team that includes personnel from many diverse sections of the company. How, then, do you give it continuity? How do you ensure that the reader will not be conscious of a lack of flow, changes in styles, gaps in development? One way is to have an editing team of two or three people work the final rough draft over from start to finish. Experienced editors can spot weaknesses, breakdowns in structure, and lack of transitions. If there is time, they can correct them. But that is always one of the major hurdles with proposals — time. Often the final rough draft is not finished until the very last moment; typing on the final is already beginning, and the fast-approaching deadline creates a panic. A careful editing job is not possible in this environment. So a better approach often is modular writing.

Modular Writing

Most proposals can be divided into modules or sections that have a certain autonomy of their own. The introduction is a module, as is the summary. In the discussion section, a unit on design requirements or a unit on product development could constitute a module. Others might be reliability, quality assurance, phasing and schedules, and the subcontractor plan. In the capabilities section, units such as related experience, personnel, and facilities could certainly be treated as separate modules.

The modules come from the outline. In the beginning stages, as the proposal team is selected, they work out an outline. When the outline is agreed upon, the proposal manager and others assign writing responsibilities. Thus, a working outline might look something like the one in Table 7–3.

Section No.	Section Title	Responsibility	Due Date
1.	Introduction	James Waters, Marketing	Feb. 15
2.	Problem Statement	Bill James, Eng. Design	Feb. 5
2.1	Mission Requirements	" "	Feb. 6
2.2	Background—Proposed Approach	" "	Feb. 6
2.3	Remote Sensing	Julie Peters, Instrumentation	Feb. 7
2.3.1.	Basic Principles	" "	Feb. 7
2.3.2.	Instrumentation	" "	Feb. 7

Table 7–3
Writing Responsibilities Are Assigned from the Proposal Outline

With a complete outline, you can begin to block out modules and submodules. The partial outline of Table 7–3 shows us that Bill James has three separate modules, as does Julie Peters.

In the preparation of the rough draft, each module should be titled and should start at the top of a new page. As modules are completed, they are brought to a central editing room where they are either tacked up on a wall or placed on a long table. In either case they are put in sequential order so that the editor or the program manager can tell at a glance which modules have been completed. As a module is removed for editing or additions, a note to that effect is left in its place. Writers and editors cooperate early on form and content so that each module is as complete as it can be. This cooperative effort includes all graphic materials, artwork, and the like. Figure 7–4 shows the physical form that Ms. Peters's assignment on remote sensing might take. Note that she has included a sketch of a proposed illustration, along with a caption, and has actually typed the text around it so that there is no doubt which lines in the text are the ones illustrated by the proposed figure.

When the cooperation between authors and editors is effective, the final editing becomes part of the overall iterative process and not a distinct, last-minute, midnight operation. Even more important, it should result in a smoother document, one which reads fluidly yet distinguishes clearly between sections.

Providing Transitions

A key to the document's coherence and flow is the transition provided between modules. There are many transitional devices available to

Figure 7–4
Example of the Physical Form of a Proposal Module in Rough Draft.

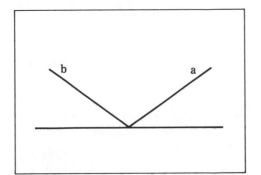
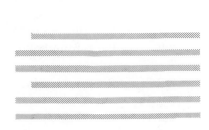

the writer and editor: pronoun references, conjunctions, transitional phrases, clauses, sentences, and even paragraphs can serve as bridges between disparate sequential ideas of various scale. The transition can come at the end of the preceding module, effectively announcing the one to follow or at the beginning of the following module, picking up the thread from the previous one.

For example, a proposal may have three modules in succession with the titles:

> Task Definition
> Work Authorization
> Cost Reporting and Control

At the end of the module on task definition is the transitional sentence:

> Thus the work release provides a detailed summary of the work performed.

At the beginning of the module on work authorization is the statement:

> The work release is submitted to the task manager and the program manager for approval.

The work authorization section concludes:

> This release, when properly endorsed, is also used to initiate funding.

The section on cost reporting and control begins with:

> A copy of the release is given to a cost analyst in the cost control group. The analyst prepares a project work request.

And so it goes. When all the modules and transitions are completed in final rough draft form, the proposal is ready for final typing and publishing as a cohesive document with a one-author look.

PRACTICAL APPLICATIONS

Exercise 1. Write the Summary of a Proposal for New Business

Select an article in a journal or a short (approximately 10 pages) report or proposal. Write a summary of it as if the document you are summarizing were a proposal for new business. The summary should be not more than one page. Remember that the summary is a digest of the proposal and should contain all the essential information in the report, including final results, recommendations or conclusions. Since the summary is aimed at the busy executive who may not have time to read the entire proposal, it must provide him with enough information so that he may gain a distinct impression of the work described in the document. (See the Guide, Chapter 11, paragraphs 11.11 to 11.18.)

Exercise 2. Try Your Hand at Modular Proposal Writing

This exercise requires that three-member groups be formed. Each group should "brainstorm" an idea upon which a Bellco proposal can be written. (See Chapter 2, Figure 2–1, for the list of Bellco projects.) Each group should perform the following steps:

1. "Brainstorm" and select an idea upon which to write.
(in-class, 20 min.)

2. Divide the proposal into three main modules: introductory material, discussion, and capabilities. Prepare a preliminary outline and schedule.
(in-class, 20 min.)

3. Each group decides on its own which member will prepare which module.
(in-class, 5 min.)

4. Each group member prepares his or her assigned material.
(at home)

5. The group meets at the next scheduled class hour and discusses the writing and adds the necessary transitions.
(in-class, 30 min.)

6. Each member types up his or her portion of the proposal to submit to the instructor.
(at home)

Exercise 3. (Optional)

Exercise 2 can be carried one step further. As a class, decide on a hypothetical amount of money your company will spend this year for proposed new ideas. In competition for the funds, each proposal team should prepare a brief presentation from the material in the proposal prepared for Exercise 2. The class represents the management of the customer company; they listen to and evaluate the presentations and select those proposals most deserving of funding. Evaluation criteria can be that the presentation is: convincing, clear, concise, and correct. Consult Chapter 5, the section on Oral Reports, for guidelines.

PART TWO ·– THE TROUBLE-SHOOTER'S GUIDE

THIS SECTION OF the book is a guide to practical writing. First, it offers suggestions about planning and organizing as one means to clear thinking and as a means to quick rough drafting. Most of these suggestions are offered in the form of questions you can ask yourself to put your thoughts and materials in order. The main point is to spend a lot of time thinking and working out what you want to say before you begin to write. Then write your rough draft as fast as you can — simply to put your thinking on paper where you can see what it looks like; then rearrange, cut and paste, juggle statements, until it comes close to what you really mean to say.

We also offer suggestions about reviewing and revising — offering checkpoints for the most common weaknesses and errors, both telling and showing the kinds of things to look out for. We suggest that you use this guide by applying it to some of the common documents (letters, proposals, reports) presented in Chapters 1 through 7.

Knowing that many companies have their own ways of doing things, we have not tried to set rigid guidelines for various common kinds of documents. Instead, we suggest that "When in Rome, do as the Romans do." If you work independently, the suggestions offered in this book should see you through any normal project. We have tried to answer the question: What are the basic requirements of good practical writing?

In Part One, we looked at the kinds of writing frequently demanded in business and industry. Our chief concern in Part Two is to provide a guide to a clear, plain, and convincing style that is acceptable anywhere.

We feel that this guide and a good dictionary should be all you need to do most of the writing required of you in business and industry. We hope that as you leave school and enter business this book will find a place on your desk, ready for use as a handy reference. It is designed to serve this function for years to come.

ORGANIZING AND PLANNING ☞

8

METHODS OF ORGANIZING

8.1   An old recipe for rabbit stew begins: "First catch the rabbit." The same principle applies to writing: first have something to say. If you do know what you want to say but just can't get started, try drawing sketches or making lists.

Try Sketching a Model

8.2   Figures 8-1, 8-2, and 8-3 show three kinds of sketches that help to organize ideas.

8.3   The first, a sketch of classification, shows graphically that both the lower elements are forms of the upper element. Perhaps the person who drew Figure 8-1 started with the subject of radiation: he wrote out the word, circled it, then put its counterpart, conduction, in another circle. That reminded him that, after all, both are methods of heat transfer. Looking at this classification, he realizes that he can explain the radiation he is required to write about in terms of the concept of heat transfer. He

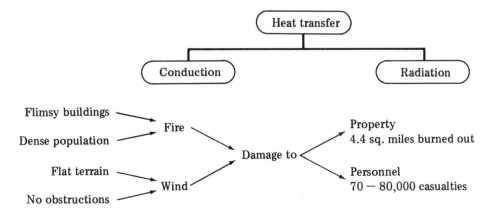

Figure 8-1
*Sketch of Classi-
fication.*

Figure 8-2
*Sketch Showing
Cause and Effect.*

might even find it useful to bring in the idea of conduction, explaining how it does or does not apply to the radiation that is his subject.

Figure 8-2 is a sketch that shows cause and effect. Suppose that the student who drew this one had as her assignment the task of explaining what relationship, if any, there is between topography and the extent of fire damage that occurs annually in the United States. It seems probable that her diagram of the causes that contribute to fire damage is going to lead her to determine that topography does influence fire damage.

Figure 8-3 is a graphic representation of a procedure. It is more useful than a list would be because it reminds the "artist" and the reader that the procedure is circular: one can begin anywhere in the chain of tasks and work in either direction. Certainty about the condition of the machinery can be attained only by carrying out all the tasks, but there is no required order for the work.

8.4

8.5

Try Listing and Classifying

Simply list everything you can think of — as you think of it. Once you've run out of things to write, look over your list, seeking common denominators as a basis for classification.

Classification means grouping things according to similar characteristics — such as grouping the fifty states by geography, or by size, or by population, or by money spent on education, etc. Classes are broken down into subclasses, which also are formed on the basis of some shared similarity. Both classes and subclasses can be put in rank order according

8.6

8.7

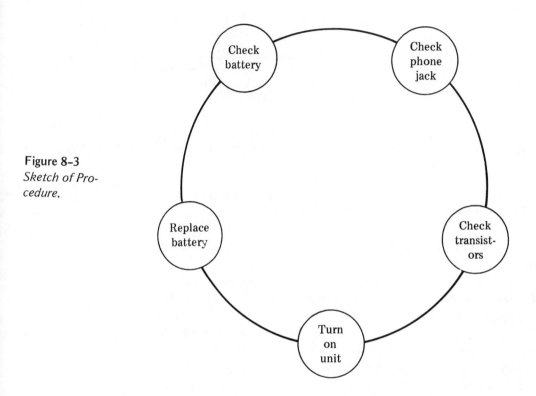

Figure 8–3
Sketch of Procedure.

to their relation to the largest entity. A common form of classification is the familiar organization chart. (See Figure 8–4.)

8.8   A typical application of a list is the biographical résumé submitted with a letter of application. (Résumés are discussed in detail in Chapter 1.) From everything about your life, you make a list of anything that would interest a prospective employer. Start by listing everything you can think of:

    References
    Licenses
    Honors
    Citizenship
    Marital Status
    Birthdate
    Birthplace
    Address

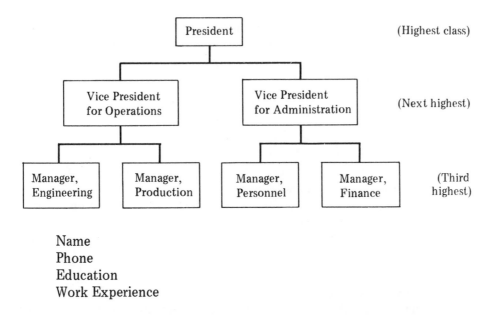

(Highest class)

(Next highest)

(Third highest)

Figure 8-4
*The Organization
Chart as a Classi-
fication Medium.*

Name
Phone
Education
Work Experience

Then classify the items, grouping the *kinds* of information into classes
(Personal Data, Education, Professional Experience, Honors and Awards,
References). Rank the classes according to how important they would be
to the prospective employer.

What comes first depends on whether the position is for someone
fresh out of school (in which case Education would come first) or for
someone with experience (in which case Professional Experience would
come first). In some cases, Honors and Awards could come next — especially if the position involves considerable public relations work. For any
purpose, references commonly come last. As always in the process of organizing, the selection and arrangement of most elements must be adjusted
to the topic, the purpose, and the reader.

8.9

Try a Flowchart

To show a cause-effect relationship, a flowchart is excellent because
it indicates movement in time: one thing happens *as a result of* something
else having happened. (See Figure 8-5.)

8.10

Figure 8-5
*A flowchart can
Show Cause and
Effect.*

8.11   To show a step-by-step procedure, a flowchart is effective because it shows *what must be done before something else can be done.* Charts can be designed so as to show which steps can be performed as alternates or at the same time.

STEPS IN PLANNING

8.12   All activity in business and industry eventually becomes a matter of record, so it makes sense to think of writing as part of any program plan.

8.13   Most large companies employ professional writers to prepare final reports, brochures, or proposals. But they prepare these documents from reports submitted by the various departments. This "input" is prepared by nonprofessionals and it follows the rule for computer input — "Garbage in, garbage out" — that is, a report is only as good as the input that goes into it. Therefore, even if you are not responsible for the finished report and are supplying only a small portion of it, whatever you supply can make the difference between a strong and weak product. Writing is a part of your job!

8.14   While your main concern is with completing your assignment, you ought to analyze the writing portion of the work in the same way that you analyze the requirements of the total task.

Analyze Your Assignment

8.15   1. What is the *aim* of the work? What problem will it solve? What question will it answer? What need will it fill?

2. What is the *immediate purpose?* Will you compile data, analyze it, derive conclusions, make recommendations?

3. What is the *scope* of the work? Is this the whole task or only a part of a larger program? How will your portion fit into work that has already been done and will be done in the future? What specific tasks must be completed?

4. How will *the work be scheduled?* Who will do what, where, when, how? What materials must be obtained? What equipment? What tasks must be done before the actual work can begin? Which tasks must be completed before other tasks begin? Which tasks can be carried on at the same time and in the same place?

5. How will *the writing be scheduled?* What writing must be done? Who will do it? When? What parts can be written beforehand? Which parts must be completed before other parts can be started? (See the sample writing schedule in Figure 8–6.)

Quality Environment Division

SAMPLE PLAN

AIM: To survey what has been done to shield residential areas from factory noise.

The Problem: Federal law requires factories with
more than 20 employees and with government contracts in excess of $10,000 to limit maximum
noise levels to 90 db. This is 5 db above acknowl-
edged safety limits. Our problem is to shield
this hazardous noise so that the level in nearby
residential areas rises no higher than 85 db.

IMMEDIATE PURPOSE: We already know that some states
have laws more strict than the government regulations, and that Russia has had stringent regulations since the early sixties. Our immediate
purpose, then, is to survey the literature on
shielding noise.

SCOPE: Our work will be limited to this literature
survey in search of proposed approaches and
proven solutions developed by companies in circumstances similar to our own.

Figure 8–6
Analysis of the Writing Assignment.

APPROACH: Jane Pederson, a writer in Bellco's publication department, will do the research in the
company library from 11 January to 28 February.
The basic text will be Karl D. Kryter, <u>Effects
of Noise on Man</u> (1970), especially the bibliography, pp. 591-633. This will provide an overview of work published through 1970. Reference
personnel in the library will provide an updated
list of publications since that time. In addition, Ms. Pederson will correspond with other
firms in our circumstances -- Ramage Steel,
Johnson Corporation, and Vital Industries. She
also plans field trips to these firms during the
early weeks of February.

Figure 8-6
Continued

SCHEDULE:

Start	Complete	Task
1/4/	1/11/	1. Preliminary survey of Kryter text. 2. Library staff updates Kryter text.
1/12/	2/1/	3. Prepare abstracts of pertinent articles. (library staff) Concurrent correspondence. (Pederson)
2/2/	2/14/	4. Field trips to Ramage, Johnson, and Vital. 5. Prepare three trip reports. (Pederson)
2/15/	2/28/	6. Analyze abstracts. (Pederson) 7. Analyze trip reports. (Pederson) 8. Prepare summary report. (Pederson) 9. Submit report - 2/28/75.

In the sample plan shown in Figure 8-6, one person is responsible   8.16
for the entire project. She must rely on the library staff, however, to prepare abstracts. Thus she must provide the staff with a copy of her schedule
for their compliance. Likewise, she must clear the field trips with the respective firms as well as with her supervisor. Note, too, that she has
scheduled four writing tasks — three trip reports and a summary report.
Normally a firm plan of this kind requires approval from her supervisor,
Catherine Robbins, the manager of Publications, and the supervisors of
people (like the library staff) from other departments who will be engaged
in the work. It would also require firm estimates of costs for time and
materials or services.

Analyze the Requirements of the Document

1. Establish the *focal point* of the document. Should the emphasis   8.17
be on the problem or on the solution or on the procedures? Will recommendations be required?

2. Clarify the *purpose* of the document. Quick information to answer
a question? Routine report of status or progress? Formal report to complete a program of work? An instruction sheet? A description of equipment or process?

3. Limit the *scope* of the document. Should it cover everything
known about the subject, or only certain parts? Will it be an entire document in itself, or only part of a larger document? What should be included?
What should not be included?

4. Who will be the *readers?* Top management? Staff management?
Technicians? Specialists? What do they already know? What do they want
to know? What do they need to know?

5. How will the document be *used?* For quick information? For
study? For reference? For training programs or public information? As a
basis for decision?

6. Prepare a *detailed plan* for the document. Your plan could consist of a preliminary checklist:

1. Collect information.
2. Choose the appropriate report form.
3. Prepare an outline with main and chief subheadings.
4. Rough-draft the introduction, discussion, conclusion.
5. Prepare a table of contents and summary as a check on arrangement, consistency, and relevance.

6. Prepare such supplements as appendixes, bibliography, letter of transmittal, photos, and curves.
7. Review and revise the rough draft.
8. Prepare final copy.
9. Proofread.
10. Submit.

7. Chart the target dates for each phase in writing the report. (See Table 8–1.)

8.18   In a complicated report, each phase (such as writing the introduction or assembling pertinent photographs) could be broken out with a separate bar on the schedule, along with names of the persons assigned the responsibility for each task. All important tasks must be clearly marked. An honest estimate of target dates is necessary to ensure a workable schedule.

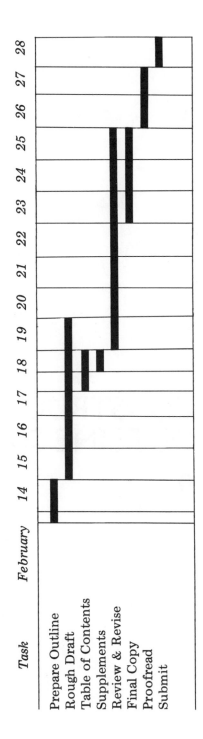

Table 8-1
Target Dates for Each Phase in the Writing

CONSTRUCTING AN OUTLINE ☞
9

Many professional writers do not use outlines. They are so familiar with formats (standard arrangements of reports) that they work from the kind of sketches we discussed at the opening of Chapter 8. In fact, it is the exceptional writer who uses the completely detailed kind of outline taught in high school.

9.1

AN OUTLINE IS A GUIDE TO SELECTION AND SEQUENCE

This section contains suggestions about the principles involved in outlining the most common kinds of documents in practical writing. When you become familiar with them from practice, you too may find yourself working from mere sketches.

Outlining is an extension of "Organizing and Planning." It allows you to *see* information in a logical sequence or relationship. Five short steps

9.2

are presented here which should help you in preparing memos, proposals, and reports.

1. Compose a target statement.
2. List supporting or explanatory points.
3. Use a familiar sequence.
4. Adjust your sequence to your purpose.
5. Adjust your sequence to your reader.

COMPOSE A TARGET STATEMENT

9.3   Sometimes a target statement is called a thesis sentence, or a topic sentence; it should be a statement that covers everything you will talk about. Think of your target statement as the headline of a newspaper. It should be as specific as you can make it at this stage — and promise no more than you can deliver. That is why it should not be too broad. Recall the principles of classification discussed at the beginning of Chapter 8 (Figures 8-1 and 8-4; paragraphs 8.3, 8.6, and 8.7). Make sure you have broken down a large class or family into the specific subclass you will cover.

9.4   For example, "Electrocardiograms" is much too broad a title and much too large a class to cover in a small report. Break it down into subclasses such as:

How to Take Cardiograms

or

How to Transmit Cardiograms by Phone.

Then write your report on this more manageable topic.

LIST SUPPORTING OR EXPLANATORY POINTS

9.5   Use the same procedure discussed earlier for classification — write out a list in random order; look for common denominators; arrange items in classes to suit the topic, purpose, and readers.

USE A FAMILIAR SEQUENCE

Most often you will be assigned a format to follow; but if you work inde-   9.6
pendently, your best procedure is trial and error: try different arrangements of supporting data until you find the optimum sequence.

      Your readers will expect to find certain kinds of information in cer-   9.7
tain places. If you are working without a prescribed format, you can rely
on these common sequences to suit the given type of topic:

For Narrative, list events as they occur or as they should occur.   9.8
                topic: servicing the snorkle
1. Removing canister assembly.
2. Removing regulator assembly.
3. Recharging cylinders.
4. Replacing orifice assembly.

For Explaining, go from the familiar to the less familiar, the nontechnical   9.9
to the more technical, the general to the specific. Use at least one example
per point.
             topic: exploring alternative energy sources
1. Solar cells.
2. Shale.
3. Nuclear fission.
4. Geothermal wells.

For Arguing, list existing arguments on each side, then your own position.   9.10
             topic: the case against using oil additives
1. Advantages of additives:
   a. They maintain oil viscosity despite temperature change.
   b. They increase thickness of oil.
   c. Added to low-weight oil they make multiweight oil.
2. Disadvantages of additives:
   a. It's cheaper to buy a heavier weight oil.
   b. Heavier oils work just as well.
   c. Additives void new car warranties.
3. Point: Additives are needlessly dangerous to high-performance
   engines.

For Describing an object, process, or system, list an overall view of the   9.11

whole class or family it belongs to, then the features that distinguish it from other members of its group, and finally its own characteristics. List these characteristics in a consistent sequence: outside to inside, clockwise, left to right.

topic: automatic timer for time-lapse photography

1. Two-part system contains timing unit & camera tripper.
2. Tripper is activated by solenoid.
3. Timing unit has disc, motor, relays, & light receptacle.
4. Motor runs continuously.
5. Timing disc trips switch to light floodlamp.
6. Disc also activates solenoid, making exposure.
7. Exposure cuts off power to floodlamp after brief delay.

9.12   *For Discussing a Problem,* list your target statement as a question or a command or a statement of need. Then list the known causes of the prob-

Quality Environment Division

WHAT CAN BE DONE ABOUT LOSS OF SUNSHINE

1. <u>Problem</u>: Since 1964, sunshine reaching the earth
   has declined about 1.3 percent - we have been
   losing 10 minutes of sunshine daily.

2. <u>Causes</u>:
   a. Inclination of the earth shifting.
   b. Increasing energy consumption pollutes the air.

3. <u>Tried Solutions</u>:
   a. Impose regulations on pollutants; e.g.,
      aerosols.
   b. Appeal for voluntary conservation; e.g., WIN.

4. <u>Proposed Solution</u>:
   Find substitute energy sources proven clean.

Figure 9-1
*A Very Brief
Outline for a
Report.*

lem, the solutions that have been tried, and the solution that you now propose. Figure 9–1 shows a very concise outline for a government study.

For Discussing a Situation or Condition, use the sequence familiar from   9.13
outlines taught in high school. The standard format is:

TARGET STATEMENT
I.   First Supporting Subpoint or Introduction
   A. Fact supporting Subpoint
      1. Discussion of that supporting fact
      2. Important information relating to that fact
         a. Discussion of that information
         b. Additional information but less important than IA2
            (1) discussion of this additional information
               (a) discussion of that minor discussion
   B. Another fact directly supporting the Subpoint

II. Second Supporting Subpoint
   A. Fact supporting this Subpoint
   B. Another fact directly supporting this Subpoint
               etc.

ADJUST YOUR SEQUENCE TO YOUR PURPOSE

Still assuming the lack of prescribed format, we suggest that your purpose   9.14
will sometimes determine the optimum sequence of information. Whether
in memo, letter, or formal report, these are the most common purposes:

1. Describing current conditions, or status.
2. Reporting activities or progress during given periods.
3. Summarizing completed activities — as final test reports and field
    trip reports.

These functions are normally met by status reports, progress reports, and summary reports. Fortunately, each type of report has certain basic elements common to all — a summary, an introduction, a discussion, and a conclusion — which will be discussed in a later section. The sequence of these elements, however, may be adjusted to the purpose of your own report; for example:

STATUS REPORT
Introduction
Summary
Discussion
Conclusions

PROGRESS REPORT
Introduction
Conclusions
Discussion

SUMMARY REPORT
Summary
Introduction
Discussion
Conclusions

9.15   In the sample outline of the summary report (Figure 9–2), note that the section, "SUMMARY," is not numbered because it forms an independent unit that the writer intends to distribute separately, while keeping the report itself on file.

9.16   In the sample outline of the status report (Figure 9–3), the summary is an integral part of the report. From the brief outline of the report, can you determine if the office has a financial problem? If so what caused it? What is the proposed solution?

ADJUST YOUR SEQUENCE
TO YOUR READERS

9.17   You may not know exactly who they will be, but you will have a general idea of what position they hold. Except for sales letters and public relations letters, practical writing is seldom designed for the general public. Instead, it is usually aimed at one or more of four occupational levels:

BC Quality Environment Division

REDUCING SULFUR IN GASOLINE

SUMMARY

I INTRODUCTION

   A. Statement of Problem

   B. Previous Methods

   C. Development of Present Method

   D. How This Report is Arranged

II CAUSTIC & POTASSIUM CRESOLATE TREATING

   A. Process Description

   B. Laboratory Procedures

   C. Tabulated Results

III AIR CAUSTIC TREATING

   A. Process Description

   B. Test Set-Up

   C. Tabulated Results

IV BENDER & METALLIC SWEETENING

   A. Process Description

   B. Laboratory Procedure

   C. Tabulated Results

V COMPARATIVE ANALYSIS

   A. Caustic & Potassium Cresolate

   B. Air Caustic Treating

   C. Bender & Metallic Sweetening

VI CONCLUSIONS

Figure 9-2
A Sample Outline of a Summary Report.

Quality Environment Division

NEW YORK DISTRICT OFFICE FINANCIAL STATUS

I. INTRODUCTION

    A. Purpose of the Report
    B. Background of the Report
    C. Overview of New York Office Activities

II. SUMMARY

    A. Overall Financial Statement
    B. Brief Discussion of Budgets
    C. Brief Discussion of Expenditures
    D. Discussion of Unexpected, Large Expenditure

III. BUDGETS AND REVENUES

    A. Budget Not Increased Over Previous Year
    B. Revenues Showed Substantial Improvement Over
       Previous Year
    C. New York Office Extended Coverage Over
       Previous Year

IV. EXPENDITURES

    A. Expenditures Increased Over Previous Year
    B. Inflation Increased at Rate Greater Than
       Anticipated
    C. Sales Convention Held in N. Y. (Originally
       Scheduled for Washington)

V. CONCLUSION

    A. Increase in Budget Needed to Cover Costs
       1. Inflation Schedule
       2. Sales Convention Expense
    B. New Budget for Next Year Must Include
       Contingencies

Figure 9-3
A Sample Outline of a Status Report.

Top management, who are nonspecialists and are looking for an overview rather than detailed explanations.

Staff management, who combine management functions with specialist knowledge and will be looking for highlights of your conclusions, along with chief supporting data.

Specialists, who will wish to have complete conclusions and supporting
   data available for study and reference.
Technicians–Craftsmen, who will be concerned with your information as
   it affects their daily, routine activities.

The relationship of the occupational level to the sequence of practical
writing is shown in Table 9-1.

Sometimes, *where* these people work also has an influence on the   9.18
sequence you choose. The most elaborate segregation of reader types is to
be found in a large industrial firm. Its operating staff is likely to be organized as follows:

Preliminary design.   Here designers develop the design requirements,   9.19
or criteria, that specify the (a) configuration, (b) materials, and (c) performance standards of each part, component, subassembly, assembly, subsystem, and system to be produced.

Research.   Specialists investigate the state of the art (the state of   9.20
current technology) so that they keep up to date on what can be done
with various materials, methods, processes, and techniques to meet the
designers' requirements. They also develop new materials, methods, etc.
themselves.

Development.   Specialists and craftsmen work from the design re-   9.21
quirements to build a prototype "mockup" or schematic. Their main task
is to develop detailed specifications (instructions) on how to produce the
product so that it conforms exactly to the design criteria — how each part
must be built, what materials must be used, and how each part must be
tested.

Manufacturing.   Craftsmen and technicians follow the specifications   9.22
in whatever form they're delivered: "specs," blueprints, schematics, or
manuals. Any departure from these specifications must be okayed by the
designers. Quality control inspectors throughout the factory check every
stage of manufacturing to ensure that the specifications are being met. If
anyone thinks a specification can be improved, he informs the designers,
who then work it out. Meanwhile, all work meets the original specifications until workers receive official okay from design to make a change.

Marketing.   Besides being responsible for sales, service, and custo-   9.23
mer relations, marketing personnel also work closely with production
people in forecasting the needs of the company and customers. They alert
designers and development engineers to what other companies are doing.

Table 9–1
*How Readers'
Occupational
Class Affects
Sequence*

Readers	Level of Data	How Much Data	Suggested Sequence
Top Management	nontechnical general	most important conclusions and only key supporting data	CONCLUSIONS INTRODUCTION
Staff Management	semitechnical less general	all conclusions tabulated supporting data	INTRODUCTION CONCLUSIONS DISCUSSION
Specialists	technical	all conclusions all supporting data	INTRODUCTION DISCUSSION CONCLUSIONS
Technicians	technical	only that portion concerning their work	CONCLUSIONS

At the same time, they keep up with activities in their own company so that they can alert various people to the possibility of applying results from one area to the problems or needs of another area.

Tables 9–2 and 9–3 show how technical information can and should 9.24 be tailored to those who must deal with it in its written form.

Data	*Top Management*	*Staff Management*	*Specialist*
Cryoforming is named after cryogenics.	X		
It applies the principle of polymorphic transformation at low temperatures to relieve residual stresses.			X
In the hardening process, a part is heated to 1725° F then cooled to –110° F.		X	
Cryoforming achieves tolerances the thickness of a human hair.	X		
Cryoforming achieves tolerances of 0.002 in.		X	
Cryoforming achieves tolerances of 0.002 for each 12 inches of a 36-part.			X
In the hardening process, a part is cooled gradually in a solution of dry ice and trichloroethylene.		X	X
Cryogenics is the study of materials at temperatures down to –459.6° F.	X	X	

Table 9–2

Examples of Technical Information Selected for Different Kinds of Readers

| | | Order of Sentences to Suit: | |
Data	Top Management	Staff Management	Specialist
1. From 3 February to 30 July 1964, the Federal Aviation Agency subjected Oklahoma City to more than 1200 sonic booms.	1	1	1
2. This was a test program studying effects of sonic booms on structures and people.	5	2	2
3. The FAA rented 9 houses as "test houses."	6	4	3
4. Direct scientific evidence proves that the booms caused no damage to the test houses.	2	3	4
5. The FAA paid off claims by more than 200 residents for broken glass or cracked plaster.	7	8	5
6. Forty percent of 2000 homeowners interviewed were convinced their homes had been damaged.	3	7	6
7. At the start of the tests (February), 90 percent of those interviewed said they could learn to live with the booms.	8	6	7
8. At the close of the tests (July), 73 percent said they could learn to live with the booms.	4	5	8

Table 9-3
Example of Arranging Information for Different Kinds of Readers

We assume that the top management reader would not read beyond sentence 4; that the staff management reader would skip over sentence 3, and would like sentences 4–6 and 7–8 combined.

WORKING ON A ROUGH DRAFT ☞

10

10.1   This is no time to worry about word choice or sentence structure. The object now is to work out your ideas on paper, so *write as fast as you can* —preferably without interruption. Pace yourself. Work intensely for 20 minutes, then take a short break, then work another 20 minutes and break. Experiment till you find the best pace for yourself. But in your work period, keep your mind on your work, and write as fast as you can.

YOUR ROUGH DRAFT IS NOT A FINAL DRAFT

10.2   If you can't think of a word, leave a blank. If you can't decide between two words, write them both. If you have long, complicated data, leave a space and write "Insert #1," "Insert #2," etc. And don't be a slave to your outline. If a new idea comes along, work it out and change your outline.

176

THINK IN TERMS OF THREE PARTS

You need those same three parts again — a beginning, a middle, an end — in which you tell your readers what you are going to tell them, then you tell them, and finally you tell them what you have told them. 10.3

In a long document the three parts appear as the introduction, the discussion, and the conclusion. But even if your document consists of only three sentences, consider the first one an introduction, the second a discussion, and the third a conclusion. 10.4

Paragraphs also are constructed in three parts. The topic sentence covering the message of the paragraph serves as a summarizing introduction. The middle of the paragraph develops the message by discussing general and specific examples or explaining specific steps or reasons. The end of the paragraph restates the topic sentence in other words, and often refers to the paragraph that follows. Figure 10-1 shows an annotated sample paragraph. 10.5

We can see that the procedure for writing paragraphs and entire documents is essentially similar: You make a point. You support the point with an explanation. You conclude the point with a reminder of its importance. Think in terms of three parts. 10.6

	Beginning	*Middle*	*End*
Paragraph	Topic Sentence	Support	Restatement
Document	Introduction	Discussion	Conclusion

FOLLOW THREE STEPS – DISTILL, CLARIFY, EMPHASIZE

Sometimes it seems that you can dance all around a problem forever, but it's just impossible to get in and tackle it. Anticipating the struggle is always worse than the struggle itself. And in writing, too, you find the ideas seem to come out quite impressively — once you get started. 10.7

You have that outline you've done. Don't sell it short. To make the outline you had to choose a thesis, or point, figure out what you wanted 10.8

Figure 10-1
*A Sample Para-
graph.*

Quality Environment Division

Topic sentence

Two subtopics:
1. Color TV
*2. Longplay
   record*

*Subtopic 1
discussed*

*Subtopic 2
discussed*

*Conclusion, with
forecast of fol-
lowing paragraph
and echo of topic
sentence*

Peter Goldmark, now head of CBS Laboratories,
created at least two revolutions in our lifestyle.
In 1940, he built the first practical color TV system;
and in 1948, he produced the first longplaying record.
His first color system, based on a rotating disc with
a set of filters, was operational in the summer of
1940; but its development was curtailed by World War
Two. Its invention had taken only three months in
contrast to the three years he needed to develop
the longplaying record. A professional musician as a
young man, Goldmark was irritated by the clatter
the records made as each was dropped to the turn-
table by the automatic changer. He found it particularly exasperating when it interrupted the flow of
a long piece. One night in 1945, the records changed
right in the middle of a beautiful work he was lis-
tening to: "I knew right then and there I had to
stop that sort of thing." And now, with the same
sense of determination, he has developed a system of
electronic video recording for the home that promises
to create still a third revolution in the way we live.

to say about the point, and determine the most effective order for presenting those statements so that the reader would get the message you were trying to convey. You've really done all the hard work already: those were the difficult decisions.

Keep in mind three suggestions as you prepare to write your rough draft: distill, clarify, and emphasize:

10.9

1. Distill your message down to one straightforward sentence, covering the most important thing you want to say. (This was the target statement of the outline.)

2. Clarify your message with an introduction and discussion. (These were the supporting or explanatory points that made up the outline; and the outline now has them in a logical order as well.)

3. Emphasize your message with a concluding statement of what your readers should do, think, or expect to happen next. Don't look to the discussion section of your document to inspire you with a way to emphasize the message: think, instead, about your target statement. What was that single most important message you had for the reader? AND What is your purpose in writing the document? The answers to these two questions will point directly to the wording of your concluding statement.

REVIEWING AND REVISING ☞

11

R eview and revise systematically as you shape and polish your rough draft. First, skim the draft, adding headlines and subheadlines for all important points. List these headlines as a rough table of contents. Does the title of your document give a true view of the contents? Has anything important been omitted? Should anything be rearranged?

11.1

Do not worry yet about spelling and punctuation. At this point, you are checking for good sense, clarity, and concise style. Now is the time for carefully reviewing the organization and connection of the thought, the clarity and smoothness of the style. The following checklists should help you work systematically.

11.2

Review the Sense. See that your rough draft:

11.3

1. Focuses on one main point.
2. Adjusts information and language to your readers.
3. Keeps the information simple by summarizing, clarifying, and emphasizing.
4. Supplies reasons for arguments and support for generalizations.

11.4   5. Concludes by reviewing and by reminding readers about what to do, think, or expect.

Review the Expression. Then rearrange, delete or recombine material to achieve:

1. Straightforward sentences.
2. Plain words and idioms.
3. Clearcut sentences.
4. Complete thoughts.
5. Clear modifiers.
6. Correct pronouns.
7. Proper verb forms.
8. Only necessary words.
9. No needless repetition.
10. Simplified clauses.
11. Smooth continuity.

REVIEW AND REVISE THE SENSE

Focus on One Main Point

11.5   Does everything in the document have direct bearing on the title? You can check this by making a headline for each paragraph in order to summarize it, then listing the headlines. But the headlines must be specific. What good is a list that says:

Introduction
Discussion
Conclusion?

You need *specific* headings like this:

Background of Hydrogen Emissions
Factors Bearing on Hydrogen Emissions Now
Observed Instances of Emissions
Proposed Solution to Current Emissions

Requirements	Bad Examples	Good Examples
Identify the Most Important Point	Test Report of Pratching*	Pratching Circuitry Test*
Identify the Real Contents	Pratching Circuits†	Pratching Circuit Design†

Table 11-1
Meeting the Requirements of a Good Title

*The report deals with the testing of pratching circuits.
†The report talks only about the design of pratching circuits.

The headings thus provide a running summary of the document, and the title should be a general summary of the entire document. Remember that the title should promise no more than the document delivers. (See Table 11-1.)

Figure 11-1 lists some specific and well-conceived titles of Bellco Corporation documents. When you read each title thoughtfully, you realize that you have a very clear idea of what each document discusses.

11.6

Adjust Information and Language to Your Readers

To see whether your document uses information and language appropriate to the class of readers you are aiming to reach, you can use the device shown in Figure 11-2. Here is how it works:

11.7

Place the left end of a straight-edge on the left-hand vertical scale labeled *Class of Readers*, positioning it to cross that scale at the indicator for the appropriate class. Lay the right end of the straight-edge on the indicator in the right scale, *Probable Use*, which represents the way you expect the document to be read. The point at which it crosses the middle scale represents the level of language and information you should strive to achieve in your work. Thus, for example, if you are writing a document for top management which you expect them to study, you should be using semitechnical language along with tabulated facts and figures.

11.8

The way we normally adjust language and information to the people we are talking to was humorously illustrated by E. J. Tangerman, longtime editor of *Product Engineering*, as he once told us how Archimedes announced a great discovery to four different people:

11.9

To his wife: "I'm sorry I flooded the bathroom, dear, and sure I'm ashamed to run naked through the streets yelling, 'Eureka!' but don't you see, dear, the king gave me a problem to solve and

Suitable level for a layman

BC Quality Environment Division

Figure 11-1
Examples of Bell-co Report Titles.

Electronic Monitoring of Automated Postal System
Components

Survey of Interurban Rail Rapid Transit Systems in
1975 (USA)

Systems Design for Inner-City Monorail

Long-Range (10-Year) Planning for Recreational Areas
in San Diego

Cost Analysis of Modular Housing Units, Barndail Park

Design of Low-cost Teaching Machine for Paraplegics

Computerized System for Maintaining Water Quality
Control

Shake Test of Reinforced-Adobe Housing Units

Development of Atmospheric Pollution Analyzer

Methods of Deriving Activated Charcoal from Sludge

Adapting Systems Control in Health Administration

Projected Production of Power from Geothermal Sources,
1975-85

Census of Food and Drug Administration Injunctions --
Current

I'm afraid we'd lose our contract if I don't get to him in a hurry with the solution I just found. . . ."

For top management

To a ship-builder: "You have used my screw to dewater your ships and my burning glass to set fire to the Roman galleys, and my lever to move great weights by hand. Thus you know I speak the truth when I say that these mechanisms have but little importance next to a new discovery of mine by which I can weigh ships with or without cargoes. . . ."

For staff management

To an engineer: "The volume of an irregular object, as well as its composition, can be determined by two new hydrostatic principles which I shall demonstrate. The principles are: (1) A body im-

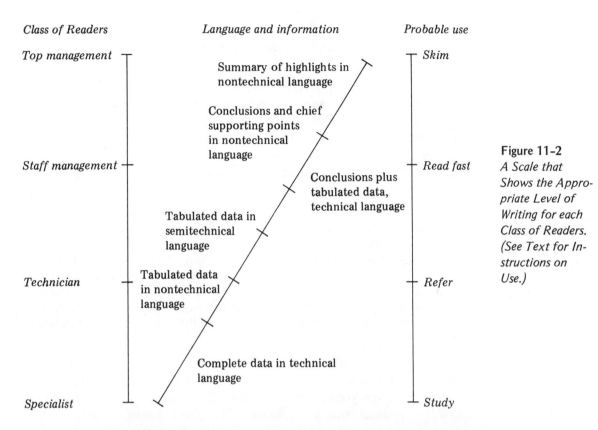

Class of Readers	Language and information	Probable use

Figure 11-2
A Scale that Shows the Appropriate Level of Writing for each Class of Readers. (See Text for Instructions on Use.)

mersed in a fluid displaces its own volume; (2) a body immersed in a fluid loses as much weight as an equal volume of the fluid."

To a mathematician: "To determine the volume of an irregular object, immerse it in fluid. The volume of the fluid displaced will be that of the object $V_1 - V_2$. Further, the body will lose as much weight as an equal volume of the fluid, thus: $W_o - W_s = W_f$."

For a specialist

The same common sense that tells you how to adjust your conversation to the people you're talking to can also help you adjust your style to your readers. *Write as you would be written to!*

11.10

Keep the Information Simple by Summarizing, Clarifying, and Emphasizing

You can't tell anyone anything that is 100 percent new to him. He has to be able to relate it to something he already knows. Your task is to

11.11

avoid confusing him with undigestible facts and, at the same time, avoid making such broad generalizations that he misses your point.

11.12   *Have You Summarized All Important Points?* By analogy with newspaper articles, your document ought to begin with the most important points: who, what, where, why, when, how, and so what? Your paragraphs ought to begin with topic sentences that cover the substance of the thought. You ought to use tables and labels for complicated data. Look at following quotation for an example of good summarizing.

*An example
of summarizing*

The test showed no conclusive correlation between TV viewing and eye trouble in school children. Clinicians examined 500 boys and girls between 7 and 12 years old, asking how many programs they watched each week, and then examining their eyes. The clinicians made a record of the nature of any eye trouble and the severity of the problems. The same general procedure was followed with a control group of 800 children from the same school who watched 25 hours of TV each week. The statistical differences were insignificant.

11.13   *Have You Clarified by Definition or Explanation?* You ought to *show* how what you are talking about is similar to what he already knows. You could define your terms, describe objects or processes, and give examples — general examples, specific examples, typical examples, and composite examples. You can even use analogies — remembering, however, that analogies only illustrate your point; they don't prove it.

11.14   Let's look at some ways of clarifying information.

*Clarification by
defining*

A household is defined as including all the persons who occupy a dwelling unit. It includes related family members and also unrelated persons, such as roomers, who share the unit. Not all households necessarily contain a family, and some may contain more than one family.

By describing

A sound level meter is a simple device with a microphone, an amplifier, and an output meter. It bears four scales marked A, B, C, and C + 30, which account for all the frequency weighting networks. The A scale is the one most commonly used, and readings are given in dbA.

This index distinguishes between "project" and "event." A project is a significant effort or program which results in a particular activity. Projects are designated by a six-digit number: for example, 000191. An event is a specific occurrence which takes place as part of a project. Events are designated by the six-digit project number followed by a dash and three more digits: for example, 000191–111.

By example

Nondigestible plant fibers in *such* foods *as* wholemeal breads and cereals are essential to nutrition, especially in an age partial to refined foods *such as* sugar and white flour; think of all the soft drinks, candy, soft white bread, and cakes we consume.

By typical example

The human eye is *a camera, with the pupil as a lens and the retina as the film.*

By analogy

Have You Emphasized What's Important? Show that some things are more important than others by devoting more space to the important points or by actually saying they are "more important."

11.15

Exercise extreme caution so as not to drive the amplifier beyond the prescribed levels, as this action will result in the heating of the plate of the tubes to virtual incandescence and undesirably alter their operating characteristics.

Example of everything having equal importance

Overloading the amplifier will ruin the tubes.

Revision

Emphasis is a matter of common sense. Imagine coming home from work late at night. You park the car and notice someone has left the front gate open again. You climb the front steps, remembering that you forgot to fix the loose top step last weekend. Then you notice the front door wide open. With beating heart, you cross the threshold and stop dead — chairs are knocked over, tables overturned, drawers are scattered all over. You dash to the phone: "Police? Police! As I parked the car, I noticed someone had left the front gate open again. I climbed the front steps, remembering I forgot to fix the loose step. . . ."
No.
You say: "Police? I've been robbed!" That's what we mean by emphasis — selecting only that information relevant to the point you want to make.

11.16

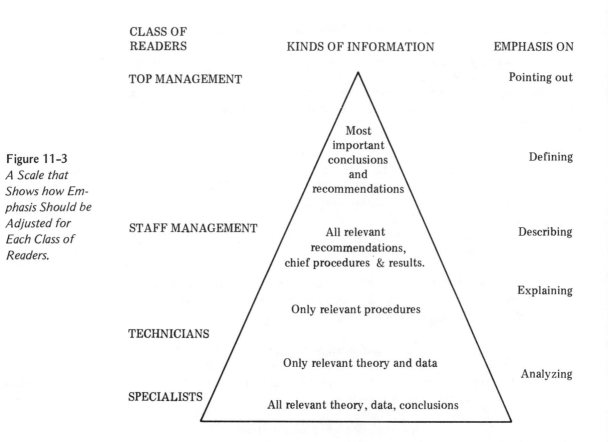

Figure 11-3
A Scale that Shows how Emphasis Should be Adjusted for Each Class of Readers.

11.17   In Figure 11-3, a chart in the form of a pyramid shows what kinds of information generally appeal to which classes or readers. It also indicates what approach should be emphasized in presenting the material. For instance, top management wants to know the conclusions and recommendations of the document so that they can make decisions based on the information. The emphasis of material directed to top management should be to point out the main facts that led to the conclusions and recommendations.

11.18   The following quotation is another good example of writing that contains no major emphasis. Every statement has equal weight, and consequently it is difficult for the reader to discover the significance of the piece.

Nineteen communicable diseases now controlled by vaccines are: cholera, German measles, infection of the adenoids, diphtheria, influenza ("flu"), mumps, measles, polio, rabies, smallpox, tetanus, typhoid, typhus, Rocky Mountain spotted fever, scarlet fever, staph infection, tuberculosis, yellow fever, whooping cough. Two infectious diseases are among the top 10 leading causes of death in this country. These are meningitis and pneumococcal pneumonia. A new vaccine is being tested for pneumococcal pneumonia. The tests are concluding now at the University of Pennsylvania and the Lilly Company, and at this time results make it appear that the vaccine will be 80 percent effective in wiping out this dread disease.

Example of everything having equal importance

When the preceding paragraph is revised, it is done with the knowledge that its new readers will represent several different classes of employees. Its various paragraphs are rewritten with that knowledge in mind.

11.19

Clinical tests of a pneumonia vaccine show that it may prove 80 percent effective in controlling one of the remaining infectious diseases among the 10 leading causes of death in the United States.

Revised for top management

Researchers at the University of Pennsylvania and the Eli Lilly Company have designed the vaccine from some dozen bacteria said to cause about 78 percent of pneumococcal pneumonia. Their tests, begun in 1972, should be completed by the end of this year.

For staff management

Their vaccine contains polysaccharide antigens from all the crucial dozen bacteria (listed . . .)

For technicians

Analysis of the antigens shows (analysis) . . .

For specialists

Supply Reasons for Arguments and Support for Generalizations
Your rough draft will contain statements of fact or opinion. In stating a general fact, make your point, illustrate it with examples, and conclude. In stating an argument, make your point, give reasons or evidence, and conclude.

11.20

Difference Between Argument and Generalization. An argument consists of two statements, one of which must be a *reason* for believing the other is true.

11.21

An Argument: Because the government now spends more than $10 billion a year on air and water quality, pollution control is a growth industry of great potential.

Reason

Conclusion

A generalization is a statement of fact and requires examples of verifiable evidence.

> A Generalization: Political leaders have shifted their attention from national defense to the preservation of our air and water resources.

11.22   Figure 11-4 shows the rough draft of a Bellco memo. When the author reviewed it, he realized he had not supported his arguments with reasons. The right half of the memo shows the revisions he made in the margins.

11.23   *Distinguish Three Kinds of Generalization.*

1. General statements of fact that can be proven true or false; e.g., "All the chairs in this room are broken."
2. Uniform generalizations about groups so large that they could

Quality Environment Division

TO: A. D. Belliston

FROM: James Burke

SUBJECT: Problems Resulting from Imposition of Fire-
           Retardancy Standards

Figure 11-4
Revising a Memo to Support an Argument with Reasons.

ROUGH DRAFT	REVISED TO INCLUDE REASONS
Bellco maintains that the new fire-retardancy standards for upholstered furniture should apply to cigarette manufacturers....	because it is cigarettes that cause the largest number of upholstery fires. There are now 27 patents on file for self-extinguishing

	cigarettes, and cigarette manufacturers could easily produce such a product.
We also believe that setting the standards should be delayed until the government has studied the matter further....	
	since 15 months seems to us inadequate for the thorough testing required for reasonable regulations, particularly considering the wide range of materials and designs now on the assembly lines.
And, finally, we suggest that the standards will raise costs to consumers in an already depressed market....	
	inasmuch as treating, say, the polyurethane foam for a standard overstuffed chair that now costs the manufacturer $12.50 will, under the new regulations, cost $15.20

never be observed in their entirety; e.g., "Daydreams represent repressed desires."

3. Statistical generalizations based on a sample but made to stand for a whole group; e.g., "The average Western diet now contains about 50 percent more refined sugar than it did in 1900."

General statements of fact require data to back them up. 11.24

Uniform generalizations require specific instances or examples of 11.25
appropriate *quantity* and *quality*. The larger the group you are generalizing about, the more instances you need. Common sense tells you that, in inspecting a carload of wheat, you need only a few handfuls from a few locations; while in inspecting a carload of cherries you need many more samples from many more locations.

In Figure 11-5 we can see that the two rough draft sentences, which 11.26

Digestion begins when food
is taken into the mouth.

Digestion com-
mences as soon as
food is taken into
the mouth, but meth-
ods differ in dif-
ferent animals. Car-
nivores, like dogs,
tear off chunks of
meat and swallow
them at once. Herbi-
vores, like cows,
chew for a long time,
making a fine mash,
then swallow and
regurgitate later
to chew their cud.
Man, with canine
teeth for tearing
and molars for grind-
ing, fits somewhere
in between.

Figure 11-5
*Rough Draft Gen-
eralizations are
Supplied with
Instances.*

There is a link between
digestion and emotion.

Digestion and
emotion are linked.
Sometimes even the
thought of a favor-
ite dish can make
the mouth water;
i.e., start saliva
flowing. And some-
times fear stops
saliva from flowing
and the tongue feels
stuck to the roof of
the mouth. Thus the
flow of a vital
digestive juice,
saliva, depends in
large part on feeling.

were generalizations, were greatly improved upon after a sensible review. The revision provides support for the generalizations by giving examples.

11.27   *Statistical generalizations* must be based on adequate sampling of a representative cross-section. The size of the sample, as for uniform general-izations, will be determined by the nature of the class you are generalizing about, the detail of analysis desired, and the variety of the cases involved. But the rules are:

11.28   *A sample is of adequate size when an increase in number of cases fails to produce significant differences in results.*

11.29   *Sampling must be based on a representative cross-section that bal-ances elements of all subgroups in proper proportion.*

Generalization: Motorists represent 13 percent of total energy use.

Users of Energy	Percentage of Use
Residential & Commercial	20
Industrial	29
Electrical Utilities	26
Transportation	
Auto	13
Public, Farm, & Freight	12

Generalization: Motorists represent 28 percent of total petroleum use.

Users of Petroleum	Percentage of Use
Residential & Commercial	20
Industrial	17
Electric Utilities	10
Transportation	
Auto	28
Trucks & Buses	12
Other	13

Table 11–2
Two Examples of Generalizations Derived from Different Samples

Comparable generalizations must be based on comparable sets of statistics. 11.30

Needless to say, the decisions on sampling have to be made when the project is in the planning stages — not when you are reviewing the draft of your report on the work. The point is, though, that it is wise to review your report with an eye to the *validity* of the generalizations and the accuracy of your account of them. 11.31

Conclude by Reviewing and by Reminding Readers

The conclusion should leave no important question unanswered. The introduction raised certain questions in the reader's mind. The discussion broke those questions into parts, and now the conclusion should put those parts back together again in proper perspective: What do they point to — an approach to a solution? a recommended solution? or simply acknowl- 11.32

edgment that the problem or question remains unchanged? Satisfy the expectations you raised in the reader's mind:

1. *Recall what you told him.* Simply summarize in a sentence or two the highlights of your information:

Summarizes the previous discussion

> Because the flow of digestive juices depends in part on emotional response, food needs to be presented appealingly . . .

2. *Remind him of its importance.* You can restate your most important point in the same words or in different words, but it should be included in the conclusion as the focal point of the entire document.

Restatement of most important point

> The psychology of nutrition, thus far overlooked by educators, may help solve the problem of national obesity.

3. *Tell him what he should be doing now.* In long documents, the recommendations may be included in a separate section. But even in the shortest memo, there should be some message about what to do or think or expect to happen next — even if all the reader should expect is another memo.

> Surely in home economics classes and preferably in health classes required of all students, we ought to include the study of nutritional psychology.

REVIEW AND REVISE THE EXPRESSION

11.33   In the first half of this chapter, we looked at the elements we must consider when we review a rough draft. These elements are integral to the sense of the exposition or argument. In this second half of the chapter we will look at the wording of the document, asking questions about the style and briefly taking up the most satisfactory ways of dealing with problem areas.

Are the Sentences Straightforward?

Backward run the sentences until reels the mind.

They sent us from the Trenton warehouse three sets of carbide tips.

Smoothly should flow the stream.

Beware of sentences that seem to run backward. "Dog bites man" does not mean the same as "Man bites dog." Any reader of English expects a basic pattern in sentences: SUBJECT (naming the actor or the person, place, or thing) followed by VERB (naming the action or condition) followed by OBJECT (naming the receiver of the action) or COMPLEMENT (referring to the subject or completing the sense of the verb).

SUBJECT	VERB	OBJECT	COMPLEMENT
"Dog	bites	man."	
"Dog	bites		hard."

These key words may be elaborated, defined, or limited in meaning by MODIFIERS:

MODIFIERS	SUBJECT	MODIFIER	VERB	MODIFIERS	OBJECT
"The gentle	dog	suddenly	bit	the suspicious	man."

These modifiers may in turn be modified by other modifiers, so that a sentence could go on for pages simply by piling up modifiers, yet still make sense — provided that the subject and verb were clear at all times and the sentence moved straight ahead.

But readers today expect short sentences, with subjects, verbs, and objects or complements kept close to the beginning of each sentence, in regular sequence. Many readers take courses in speed reading in which they are trained to look for the SUBJECT-VERB-OBJECT/COMPLEMENT pattern, even ignoring MODIFIERS. Anytime you upset the pattern, you upset their expectations — as if you were to say, "The moon was jumped over by the cow." Upsetting readers' expectations is a chief source of confusion in poor writing.

CHECKPOINTS:

Is the Subject Close to the Beginning of the Sentence? Instead of "There exists a need for funds," try: "We need funds." Distinguish the

11.34

11.35

11.36

real subject of a sentence from its grammatical subject. *Who* needs the funds? We do.

11.37   Often the choice is more complicated: "*This lab* tests brazing methods that use conduction heat" answers the question, "What does this lab do?" "*Tests* of brazing methods that use conduction heat are done in this lab" answers the question, "What kind of work is done here?" "*Brazing methods using conduction heat* are tested in this lab" answers the question, "What kinds of tests are run here?"

11.38   If in doubt, about how to phrase a statement, ask yourself *what question* you are answering.

11.39   *Is the Verb Close to the Subject?* Instead of "A memo to all departments went out yesterday," try: "A memo went out to all departments yesterday." Try to keep a clear path between subject and verb. Rearrange long modifiers and especially parenthetical expressions so that subject and verb come one right after the other.

Are There Plain Words and Idioms?

11.40   *Look Out for Vague Abstractions.* "Under certain conditions of temperature and relative humidity, moisture content of the air increases oxidation of ferrous compounds" ("Iron rusts"). "Extinguish the illumination" ("Put out the lights"). The problem with the preceding two sentences is not that the words are long, but that they are so vague as to be meaningless. By nature, an abstract word like "illumination" refers to a concept, or idea, rather than to a direct sense experience, such as seeing, hearing, touching, tasting, or smelling.

Not everyone has the same mental concepts, but most readers share sense experiences. Thus, "The *situation* in the tool shed" would mean nothing, while "The *leaking roof* in the tool shed" creates a picture even for people who have never seen the tool shed.

A classic illustration of vagueness

A farmer wrote the Department of Agriculture asking if it was safe to use hydrochloric acid to clean his water pipes. The reply came: "The efficacy of hydrochloric acid is indisputable, but the corrosive residue is incompatible with metallic permanence." Gratefully the farmer wrote back his thanks, saying he would order some on Monday. Fortunately, an intelligent clerk opened his message and shot back a telegram: "Don't use hydrochloric acid. It eats hell out of the pipes."

CHECKPOINTS:

Can Abstract Words Be Changed to Concrete Words Referring to Things?   11.41

Abstract Draft	Concrete Revision
"Two positions were excessed and their responsibilities integrated."	"The chairmanships of the safety council and recreation council were absorbed by the new office of Employee Relations Chief."
"Man-machine requirements in the system environment impose severe acuity problems."	"The pilot is so draped with test equipment monitoring his health that he can barely see the instrument panel."
"Implementation of this recommendation should assist materially in fulfilling contractual requirements."	"If the tanks could be constructed on the trailers that will deliver them, they could be shipped by 15 November 1978."

Some Abstract Words to Watch for: 11.42

considerably	modification
experiences	occurrence
facility (place)	remuneration
implementation	situation
incidence	substantially
materially	utilization

Are the Sentences Clearcut?

By definition, a sentence can have only one main Subject-plus-   11.43
Predicate. While sentences often have additional Subject-plus-Predicate combinations, these are considered subordinate clauses, less important than the main Subject-plus-Predicate.

Use a comma to connect a subordinate clause to the main Subject-   11.44
plus-Predicate if the subordinate clause comes first and begins with a word like: "if," "although," "as," "when," "where," "because," "since," or "while."

Two Sentences: "The belt is frayed. Replace it."

One Sentence: "If the belt is frayed, replace it."

You *could* use a semicolon to connect two closely related sentences:

Two Sentences: "We hired Juan Foderode. He is a good worker."

One Sentence: "We hired Juan Foderode; he is a good worker."

But this weakens your style. If you must combine closely related sentences in this way, make sure that you use semicolons rather than commas:

"Parking is free; however, a validated pass is needed for entry."

"Thursday is a legal holiday; therefore, no shipments will be accepted."

"The coolant is leaking; nevertheless, the engine will run an hour longer."

"The operators are striking; consequently, we have fallen behind schedule."

Your main objective is to avoid confusion. It is possible, for example, that the first example could be read, "Parking is free however . . ." The words to beware of are:

"however"   "therefore"   nevertheless."

11.45   *Listen to the Words for Appropriateness.* You have more than one vocabulary. Some expressions that would be appropriate in highly formal writing sound ridiculous in conversation. But even in conversation we use different expressions for rapping with buddies on the street and for engaging colleagues in professional consultation. Part of acquiring sophistication is learning how to adjust to time, place, circumstance, and people. Trust your sense of what "sounds right." In writing, try for the natural, conversational language you would use in a professional phone call.

11.46   *Listen for Natural Idiom.* Many expressions in English do not make literal sense; e.g., "Put out the light" does not mean put the light out of doors. Yet it is these expressions that make style seem natural in writing as well as in conversation. Just be sure when you use idioms that you are reproducing the correct form:

corrupted idiom	*natural idiom*
cannot help but	cannot help
comply to	comply with
conform in	conform with (or to)

corrupted idiom	*natural idiom*
identical to	identical with
in accordance to	in accordance with
incapable to do	incapable of doing
in search for	in search of
in the year of 1976	in 1976
off of	off
plan on	plan to
try and see	try to see
type of a	type of

Are Sentences Complete?

A sentence fragment is a group of words punctuated to look like a sentence but lacking either a subject or a predicate — and therefore not a sentence. A fragment can be confusing because the reader has trouble telling whether the fragment belongs to the sentence before or after it. The most common fragments are phrases (a phrase differs from a clause in lacking either a subject or a predicate); there are prepositional phrases and verb phrases, both of which are exemplified in the following sentences.

11.47

> The fumes seeped into the machine shop. *Through the ventilator.* The safety inspector sounded the alarm.

Prepositional phrase as fragment

This fragment can be easily fixed by attaching the prepositional phrase to the sentence before it: "The fumes seeped into the machine shop through the ventilator." As a rule, check any sentence beginning with such a prepositional phrase, making sure it has both subject and predicate.

> The fumes seeped into the machine shop. *Being blown through the ventilator.*

Verb phrase as fragment

or

> The fumes seeped into the machine shop. *To blow through the ventilator.*

or

> The fumes seeped into the machine shop. *Expelled through the ventilator.*

Like the prepositional fragment, this kind can be fixed by attaching it to the previous sentence, except now you will normally need a comma: "The fumes seeped through the machine shop, being blown through the ventilator." As a rule, check sentences beginning with verb phrases to make sure you have both subject and predicate.

11.48   Subordinate clauses also can turn up as sentence fragments. They look more complete than phrases do, so we must be just that much more careful in checking them. Subordinate clauses, as we have seen have both subject and verb; what they lack is independence.

Subordinate clause as fragment

Our plant shut down. *Because we had a shortage of natural gas.*

This kind of fragment does have a Subject-plus-Predicate ("We had a shortage . . .") but it also has a subordinating conjunction ("Because"). It ought to be tied to the preceding sentence without a comma. Beware of sentences beginning with subordinating conjunctions:

"Because"   "Although"   "While"   "Though"

Are Modifiers Clear?

11.49   We know that all sentences are made up of a subject and a predicate. The subject is usually a noun, and the predicate is usually a verb alone or with a complement or an object — signified by N, V, and C or N, V, and O. To any of these key words may be added other words, phrases, or clauses that elaborate, describe, clarify or otherwise modify them individually or the sentence as a whole. Normally we can tell which words are being modified by the position of the modifiers in the sentence: "Only I love you." "I only love you." "I love only you." "I love you only." The general rule is that the modifier must stand close enough to the word it modifies so that the relation is clear. But any time the basic word order, N V O, is upset, we risk separating modifiers from their normal order as well.

11.50   For example, the modifier could relate to more than one word or idea:

Take a spoonful of this before you go to bed in a cup of tea.

Instead, try "Take a spoonful of this in a cup of tea before . . ."

In the parade will be hundreds of children carrying flags and many important officials.

Instead, try "In the parade will be many important officials and . . ."

When walking on the sidewalk, the lady should be on the inside of the gentleman.

Instead, try "When walking on the sidewalk, the gentleman should be closer to the curb than the lady is."

The modifier could also be too far from the word it modifies: 11.51

What did you bring that book that I didn't want to be read to out of up for?

Instead, try "Why did you bring up that book . . . ?"

Are Pronouns Correct?

When we substitute pronouns for nouns to avoid repetition, we run   11.52
the risk of confusion.

When *they* are packed in metal containers, shippers save money."

This sentence could be: "When bearings are packed . . . , shippers save money." Or it could be stated as: "When they are packed in metal containers, bearings cost less to ship."

The added feature of a safety switch, combined with ease of operation and low maintenance, makes it an attractive press. *They* will prove more economical in the long run.

The second sentence could be: Such a press will prove . . ."

Confusion produced by careless use of pronouns can easily be dis-   11.53
covered in review.

Two common problems to beware of are those resulting from (1)   11.54
separating pronouns too far from the words they stand for, and (2) confusing their grammatical form, or case.

No sample sent to the lab between March and September of last year passed environmental testing, even though *they* had passed inspection and *they* subjected them to standard test procedures *they* have always used.

This sentence could be rewritten as: "Even though *they* had passed inspection, all samples tested between March and September last year failed the standard environmental tests."

When working in high-noise environments each worker must wear *their* protective devices provided by the Company.

This sentence should be: ". . . each should wear *his* . . ."

Are Proper Verb Forms Used?

11.55   The form of a verb shows (1) tense, or when an action occurs; (2) voice, or whether the subject performed the action or was acted upon; (3) person, or who performed the action; and (4) mood, or the manner in which the writer means the action to be understood — e.g., as a wish, command, condition, or statement of fact.

11.56   Most common are those faulty verb forms resulting from carelessness, especially those in which a plural verb form is used with a singular subject, or vice versa:

Verb faults in person

Each employee on day, swing, and graveyard shifts *have* been assigned ID cards.

Such faults can be repaired by careful revision, as can mistakes in mood. The following sentence shows a common foulup of moods; we offer two acceptable ways to correct it.

Verb faults in conditional clauses

Workers will die if they came in contact with the fumes.

This can be correctly restated as either:

Workers would die if they came in contact with the fumes.

or

Workers will die if they come in contact with the fumes.

Another common fault is confusing verb tenses. Any good dictionary can help here, since it will give the basic forms for *irregular* verbs: 11.57

break / broke / broken / breaking

The basic forms for *regular* verbs are easily derived from the basic words:

call /	call*ed* /	call*ed* /	call*ing*
(present)	(past)	(past participle)	(present participle)

The basic form "call" serves to show the present tense and, with the addition of the auxiliary "will," to show the future tense. The ending -ed shows the past tense. These are the three primary tenses. The past participle combines with "has," "have," "will have," "will have had" to show whether the action was completed before another action was begun in the past or will be begun in the future. The past participle also combines with "is," "was," etc. to show whether the subject was acted upon. And the present participle uses -ing to show that the action is continuing or progressive.

Are There Any Unnecessary Words?

The most common cause of wordiness is failure to think of the right word. The difference between the right word and the almost-right word, according to Mark Twain, is the difference between lightning and lightning bug. 11.58

> In my judgment, I think that a writer when he is writing should not make use of unnecessary words that he does not need to make his point clear to whoever might read what it is that he writes.

Is the expression concise?

While an almost-right word is all right in a rough draft, you need at this point to revise it until it seems *just* right. This is especially true of simple words in idiomatic expressions ("remember the fact that" should become "remember that") or prepositional phrases ("at this point in time" should become "now"). Following is a list of common wordy expressions. The words in parentheses can be omitted, and no one will miss them: 11.59

long (period of) time
at (a distance of) 100 meters

at (a price of) two thousand dollars
(in order) to
(at a) later (date)
at a meeting (to be held) Friday
if (it is at all) possible
by (means of)

Is There Needless Repetition?

About repetition, some repetition might be effective repetition but avoid needless repetition.

11.60   Some repetition really can be effective, especially in ensuring clarity. Sometimes using a synonym or a pronoun to replace a word rather than repeat it can be like bending backward so far that you fall flat on your back. Often you can recast a sentence:

Use a synonym or a pronoun to replace a word rather than repeat a word.

That can be revised to: "Use a synonym or a pronoun to replace a word rather than repeat *it*." (Pronoun replaces "word".) The sentence can also be recast as: "Use a synonym or a pronoun to replace rather than repeat a word."

The customer said that that shipment that we thought was lost was not.

That could be recast as: "We thought the shipment was lost, but the customer said it was not." Or: "The customer said he received the shipment we thought was lost."

Some of the samples of the last batch of the paint failed testing.

That sentence should be recast as: "Some samples of the last batch of paint . . ."

The thing to do is to turn the switch to "ON" to start the motor.

That should be recast as: "Turn on the switch to start the motor" or even "Turning the switch to 'ON' starts the motor."

One way to avoid needless repetition is to remember the following: 11.61 start with the REAL subject, keep the N V O pattern, and use active verbs:

> In a sausage-skinning machine, means for rotating a sausage, means for holding a part of the skin against the rotating sausage and causing the skin to be torn off circumferentially, and means for . . . are related to one another to cause the skin to be stripped off helically.

This could easily be recast as: "A sausage-skinning machine strips the skin helically."

Are Clauses Long and Involved?

A clause contains a subject and a verb, but a phrase has only a verb. 11.62 That verb can sometimes be turned into a "verbal," which is a verb acting as a noun to take the place of the entire phrase. This is a stepdown process:

> One problem is to cut tubes *so that they will not have burrs.*

That sentence can be reduced to: "Cutting tubes *without burring* poses a problem" and even to "Cutting tubes *without burrs* poses a problem." Again, the trick is to start with the REAL subject, use the N V O pattern, and find an active verb.

Not all long clauses are necessarily weak. Sometimes a long clause 11.63 adds a certain elegance or rhythm:

> The vat contained slivers of metal *which we could not identify* but *which the Metallurgical Laboratory reported to be Titanium.*

This could be cut down to: "The vat contained unidentified slivers of metal later found to be Titanium." But the sacrifice would not be worth the effort.

Beware especially of clauses beginning with *who, which,* and *that:* 11.64

> Bill Vaughan, who is marketing representative for Loughnut Aircraft, asked for a bid by August 15.

The stripped-down version is simply: "Bill Vaughan, marketing representative for . . ."

The milling facility, which was established to speed production, enhanced our capability.

This could be: "The milling facility, established to speed production, . . ."

Please read the parts list that is enclosed.

The revised version says only: "Please read the enclosed parts list."

Does the Thought Flow Smoothly?

11.65   Just because your sentences are easy to read does not mean your paragraphs flow easily. Your thoughts need connections, even in such simple statements as:

Harry is shorter than George. Harry is taller than Willie. George is taller than Harry.

This could be made much simpler: "George is taller than Harry, who is taller than Willie."

11.66   Connecting words should be near the beginning of a sentence to show its connection to the preceding sentence or to the development of the paragraph:

If
For example
This is also
But
Furthermore
(a pronoun substituting for the subject of the preceding sentence)
(an "echo word" repreated from the preceding sentence; e.g., "That pratching valve . . .")

11.67   We have already discussed the importance of having paragraphs flow smoothly, one after the other. In Chapter 10, "Working on a Rough Draft," the emphasis was on ensuring that the document you are writing has a beginning, middle, and conclusion. But a point was made in that discussion that bears repeating here: subsections of documents have the same structure of beginning, middle, and end; and so do paragraphs and even sentences.

The rules that guide us in constructing a document of any type are basically rules of logic and simplicity. They are virtually the same for whole documents and small sections of documents. Between the logical parts there must be logical transitions as well.

11.68

CHECKING THE DETAILS ☞
12

This phase is critical. Many an otherwise brilliant document has been ruined by some error in fact or in expression that could easily have been caught by careful checking. It is imperative to:

12.1

Check for Accuracy of Data
Check for Consistency
Check for Correctness of Expression

Check for accuracy — especially of numbers and quotations. Check for consistency — so that a statement on one page does not contradict a statement on another, or the meaning of a word in one sentence does not switch when it is used in another sentence, or the spelling of a word in one place does not differ in another place. Finally, you can worry about whether these consistent forms of spelling and punctuation are *correct*.

12.2

Below is a list of common oversights. Each statement in the list demonstrates the fault it talks about; and each will be discussed in the following pages:

Use commas to prevent confusion misunderstanding and mistakes.

Its important in everyones writing to use apostrophes right.
Consult the dictionary to avoid mispelling.
Check to see if you any words out or other typographial errors.

12.3   The best rule here is REREAD AND PROOFREAD!

USE COMMAS TO CLARIFY MEANING

12.4   (For a complete list of rules governing commas, consult the Government
            Printing Office *Style Manual*, rev. ed., 1973, pp. 135-137.)

12.5   Use commas to show omission of a word or words.

He came, he saw, he conquered. (He came *and* he saw *and* he
conquered.)

It was a long, hard night. (It was a long *and* hard night.)

A. D. Belliston serves as Chief, Research. (. . . as Chief *of* Research.)

USE APOSTROPHES PROPERLY

12.6   Apostrophes show that nouns are possessive or that a word is a contrac-
            tion made up of two words. In each case, the apostrophe signifies that
            something has been omitted. In the case of possession:

John's book = John *his*   the tree's growth rate = the tree *his*
                book   growth rate.

This practice is a holdover from the days when people used the word "his"
to show possession, even if the possessor they were talking about was a
woman or a house. That is why the practice may seem illogical in some
sentences using possessives:

Everyone should lay his cowboy boots and petticoats neatly in his
drawer.

When apostrophes signify contraction, the reasoning behind the new form is not so controversial: 12.7

it's = it *is*   can't = can*not*.

Most common errors arise from confusion about personal pronouns in the possessive case. Since most nouns form possessives by adding 's, some people think personal pronouns act the same way. But personal pronouns do not need 's because they show possession by changing form: 12.8

I	→	mine
you	→	yours
he	→	his
she	→	hers
it	→	its
we	→	ours
they	→	theirs

AVOID SPELLING ERRORS

The trouble with spelling is rules. The trouble with spelling rules is that most of them were made in the eighteenth century according to the pronunciation of that time. Language has changed, but the rules change slowly. The best we can do in this *Guide* is offer a few tips on the rules, along with a list of ten words most commonly misspelled. These ought to be *memorized*. But first, the tips: 12.9

1. Try to pronounce a word correctly, since most are spelled as they sound: resistance, resistant, athlete, athletic, government.

But beware of words that sound alike though spelled differently:

affect-effect   passed-past
capital-capitol   pane-pain
close-clothes   plane-plain
complement-compliment   principal-principle
council-counsel   profit-prophet

due-do-dew   read-red
foreword-forward   ring-wring
hear-here   right-rite-write
its-it's   sail-sale
knew-new-gnu   scene-seen
know-no   scent-sent-cent
lead-led   so-sow-sew
mare-mayor   some-sum
more-mower   their-there-they're
not-knot   to-too-two
one-won   wait-weight
our-hour   weather-whether

2. Try to visualize silent letters or letters that sound as if they ought to be some other letter (the "E" in "English" sounds like an "I.").

sa*l*mon   acc*i*dent   *E*nglish   ama*teu*r

3. Look at the difference between roots, prefixes, and suffixes of words. The root is the core form of the word. The prefix is the syllable before the root, and the suffix the syllable after the root.

root: spell   *prefix:* mis-   *suffix:* -ing   *word:* misspelling

Most words retain the spelling of *prefixes* intact:

*dis*satisfied   *un*necessary   *ac*countable

But many words change the root form when suffixes are added. Normally the spelling would remain the same if the suffix begins with the SOUND of a consonant:

normal*ly*   tinc*ture* ("u" has the sound of "you")   *but* tru*ly*

And when the suffix begins with a vowel SOUND, the root changes in order to retain the sound of its own vowels:

"writing" comes from write+ing *but* "written" comes from write+en which if spelled "writen" would have the same "i" sound as "writing";

"writer" comes from write+er and so sounds like "writing" rather than "written," and is spelled accordingly "writer," with one "t."

Thus *some* roots ending in -e drop the ending to protect internal sound:

coming   desiring   admirable   codify   *but*   changeable

Any good dictionary will show how a word is constructed from root, prefix, and suffix. When you look up the word, try to see how the prefix or suffix affects its spelling. That will help you to understand the spelling and to remember it more easily.

4. Look also at the derivation of words, given in good dictionaries. If you see that "occasion" comes from a Latin prefix sometimes spelled "oc-" and a root "cadere," you may understand why the "c" is doubled. Or, if you're confused by "affect" and "effect," the good dictionary will show how "affect" uses the same prefix as "affix" plus the Latin root for "carry" — thus "to carry *to* something" is different from "effect," meaning "to carry *out* something" (or, when used as a noun, "something carried out"). "Affect" talks about a cause leading *to* a result or an effect. "Effect," as a verb, talks about bringing something out, as in "effecting a reconciliation between two parties in conflict."

Ten Words Most Commonly Misspelled
1. accessible
2. accommodate
3. acknowledgment
4. all right
5. indispensable
6. irrelevant
7. judgment
8. liaison
9. privilege
10. supersede

Common Roots
Root   *as in*

aer (air) aerate
ann (year) annual, perennial
arch (chief) architect

brev (short) abbreviate
chroma (color) polychrome
chron (time) synchronous
dat (given) data
duc (lead) ductile
dyn (power) dynamometer
fac (make) manufacture
fin (end, limit) define
flex (bend, turn) flexible
form (form, shape) deform
frac (break) refractory
gen (born) hydrogen
geo (earth, ground) geology
graph (write) telegraph
hydro (water) hydroplane
loc (place) locate
log (word, science) geology
man (hand) manual
med (middle) intermediate
metr (measure) meter
mis, mit (send) mission, submit
phono (sound) phonograph
photo (light) photograph
port (carry) transport
pyro (fire) pyromaniac
tac, tang (touch) tangent, integer
tech (craft) technical
temp (time) temporary
therm (heat) thermometer
thesis (put, place) synthetic
trac (drag, draw) subtract

Common Prefixes

Prefix   *as in*

a- (not) achromatic
ab- (not) abnormal
ad- (from) absence

a-, ac-, ad-, af-, al-,
an-, ap-, as-, at- (to or toward)
    around, accept, adore
    affect, alleviate, announce,
    approve, assimilate, attire
alti- (height) altimeter
ambi-, amphi- (both, double)
    ambidextrous, amphibious
ana- (up, back, thoroughly)
    analysis
ante-, anti- (before)
    antecedent, anticipate
ant- (against) antagonist
auto- (self) autobiography
bene- (well) benefit
bi- (two) bisexual
bio- (life) biology
circum- (around) circumstance
co-, col-, com-, con-, cor-, coun-
    (with) cooperate, collect,
    combine, concentrate, correlate,
    counsel
contra-, counter- (against)
    contradict, countermand
de- (from) detach
dia- (through) diameter
dis-, di- (apart) disagree, divide
du- (two) dual, duet
ec-, ex- (out of, away) exit, eccentric
en- (in) encyclopedia
equi- (equal, alike) equidistant
extra- (beyond) extraordinary
hemi- (half) hemisphere
hetero- (several) heterosexual
holo- (whole) hologram
homo- (alike) homogeneous
hyper- (above, more than) hyper-
    sensitive

hypo- (below, less than) hypodermic
ig-, im-, in-, il-, ir- (not) ignore,
    impossible, injustice, illiterate,
    irresponsible
in- (within) inside
infra- (below) infrared
inter- (between) interstate
intra- (within) intrastate
intro- (into, within) introduce
iso- (equal) isometric
macro- (great) macrocosm
mal- (bad) maladjusted
mani- (many) manifold
mega- (large) megacycle
meta- (changed, after, behind,
    above) metamorphosis, meta-
    physics, metathorax, metapsy-
    chosis
metro- (mother) metropolis
micro- (small) microscope
mis- (wrongly) mistake
mono- (one) monotone
multi- (many) multicolor
n-, ne- (no, not) never, neither, nor
non- (not) nonessential
o-, ob-, of-, op- (against) omit,
    object, offense, opponent
omni- (all) omniscient
out- (out) outlook
over- (more than) overestimate
pan- (all) panorama
para- (beside) paramedic, parallel
per- (through) perceive
peri- (around) perimeter
poly- (many) polychrome
post- (after) postgraduate
pre- (before) prerequisite
pro- (in behalf of) procure

proto- (first) prototype
re- (back, again) return, rewrite
retro- (backward) retroactive
semi- (half) semicircular
suc-, sub-, suf-, sug-, sum-, sup-, sus-
     (under) succession, substance,
     suffer, suggest, summary,
     suppress, suspend
super- (above) superintend
sur- (above) surface
sym-, syn- (with, together) sympa-
     thy, synthetic
tele- (far) television
trans- (across) transit
tri- (three) tripod
ultra- (beyond) ultraviolet
under- (under, less than) undersold
uni- (one) universal
via- (way, road) viaduct
with- (away, against) withdraw,
     withhold

Numbers

1	uni-, mono-
1½	sesqui-
2	bi-
3	tri-, ter-
4	quadr-
5	quinque-, pent-
6	sex-, hex-
7	sept-, hept-
8	oct-
9	non-, nov-
10	deca-, dece-
11	hendeca-, undec-
12	dodeca-, dudec-
20	icos-

```
100      cent-
1000     mill-
10,000   myria-
100,000  mega-
```

```
one-millionth     micro-
one-thousandth    milli-
one-hundredth     centi-
one-tenth         deci-
one-half          semi-, demi-
```

Common Suffixes for Nouns
Suffix   *as in*

-dom (state, condition, power)
    kingdom, wisdom
-er, -or (one who) actor, driver
-ess (female who) actress
-hood (state, condition) neighbor-
    hood
-ion (act or result) solution,
    pollution
-ism (belief) Americanism
-ist (one who believes) anarchist,
    terrorist
-ity (quality of) liberty, unity
-ment (act of, that which) conceal-
    ment, sediment
-ness (quality of) wetness, witness
-th (quality of being) warmth,
    wealth
-tue (quality of, that which) virtue,
    statue
-tude (quality of being) magnitude
-ure (quality of) stature
-us (state or condition) status
-y (act of, condition) usury, misery

Common Suffixes for Verbs

Suffix   *as in*

-ate (become or make) graduate,
    celebrate
-ish (make or bring) finish
-fy (make) unify
-ite (make) unite
-ize (make) terrorize

Common Suffixes for Adjectives

Adjectives single out — modify — nouns or pronouns (*this* man; a *hairy* one) and show their quality or condition (low, cold, numerous). Many words are made into adjectives by such suffixes as are given below. But when they are used in comparisons, they show a change in degree by a change in form (*great, greater, greatest*) or by means of the words *more* and *most, less* and *least*. Avoid comparing adjectives both ways: do not, for example, write "more better." Common adjectives that change form radically include:

bad	worse	worst
good	better	best
little	less	least
late	later	latest or last
much or many	more	most
near	nearer	nearest or next

Suffix   *as in*

-able, -ible (able to be) flexible,
    usable
-al (in the nature of) terminal,
    accidental
-ant, -ent (having the quality of)
    reliant, eminent
-ar (in the nature of) tabular, polar
-ary (having the quality of) honorary

-ate (having the quality of) pas-
    sionate
-ed (having the quality of) rusted
-en (having the quality of) broken
-ful (in the nature of) careful
-ic (in the nature of) specific
-id (having the quality of) fluid
-ine (having the quality of) crystal-
    line
-ing (in the nature of) crying
-ish (having the quality of) greenish
-ive (having the nature of) massive
-less (lacking) hopeless
-ly (like) friendly
-ory (in the nature of) contributory
-ous (full of) dubious
-some (having the quality of)
    troublesome
-y (characterized by) windy

Common Suffix for Adverbs: -ly

Adverbs single out verbs to show how, where, when, and to what degree actions are performed. But since they also can show a degree of quality (*much, well, fine*) adverbs sometimes look like adjectives. Common sense is the test: "He smells bad" (adjective) does not mean the same as "He smells badly" (adverb); "He feels good" does not mean the same as "He feels well" (adverb). The suffix -ly commonly changes adjectives to adverbs (*bad* to *badly*) and nouns to adverbs (*day* to *daily*).

Some adverbs have the same form as prepositions ("He looked about."):

about	above	across	after	against	along	around
before	behind	below	beneath	beside	between	beyond
by	down	in	inside	like	near	off	on	out
outside	over	past	since	though	throughout	to
underneath	up	upon	within	without		

The test is whether the word is describing action (adverb) or merely indicating direction (preposition). Even when the preceding words are used as adverbs, their form does not change: they do not take the suffix -ly or any other suffix.   12.10

CHECK FOR OMISSIONS AND TYPOGRAPHICAL ERRORS

One of the weakest excuses is to blame typographical errors on your typist. Typists and printers usually reproduce what you give them. (And when they do not, the error may be theirs; but since the document is yours, you are responsible for finding it and getting it corrected.)   12.11

It is your job to proofread for *accuracy* and *clarity*. Beware especially of little things like words or letters omitted or mixed up ("To err is humam"):

wife	*instead of*	life	in	*instead of*	on
sweat		sweet	fake		make
bust		bush	whore		where
fat		far	screwd		shrewd
nuns		nuts	on		or

Otherwise, you may have statements like: "Their onion was blessed with child," or "Look before you leak," or "We have contacted Hughes Stool Co."

Look out, also, for statements that could be taken more than one way. Their ambiguity could be caused by individual words or by the way the words are put together.   12.12

Without changing shape, the designers gave the brackets greater strength.

Revised, it reads: "Without changing the shape of the brackets, the designers gave them greater strength."

This is a precision computer for the wrist with easily replaced batteries.

Revised, this sentence reads: "This precision computer for the wrist has easily replaced batteries."

The Brown Shoe Company plant has about 50,000 square feet.

Revised, it reads: "The Brown Shoe Company plant has about 50,000 square feet of space."

A PRACTICAL APPLICATION OF THE MATERIAL IN THE TROUBLESHOOTER'S GUIDE

You have applied parts of the Guide to problems and exercises throughout Part I. Now the following application will allow you to apply it in a step-by-step fashion to an entire writing assignment. At first, you may feel you are spending too much time on preparation and planning and not enough time on writing. But as you become more familiar with the process, you will find that organization and planning come more easily to you. As that occurs, your writing, too, will become more logical, more direct, and, as a consequence, more convincing.

The Assignment: Write a Memo for the President

The statistics in Table 12–1 were released early in 1977. Mr. Belliston, who has always been very conscious of affirmative action, was very upset upon seeing the data. He felt that the company was not putting enough emphasis on increasing the number of female workers in management, technical, and sales areas.

He has authorized you to review and analyze the data. You are to write him a memo in which you describe the problem and recommend possible courses of action the company might take to alleviate the situation. You may not think that a problem exists. If that's the case, say so in writing, but be sure to support your contentions.

Job	Year	All Employees*	Male		Female	
			Number	Percentage	Number	Percentage
Managers	1976	4,242	4,153	97.90	89	2.10
	1975	4,290	4,223	98.44	67	1.56
	1974	4,065	4,017	98.82	48	1.18
	1973	4,115	4,075	99.03	40	0.97
	1972	4,330	4,288	99.03	42	0.97
Engineers	1976	4,275	4,048	94.69	227	5.31
	1975	4,006	3,830	95.61	176	4.39
	1974	3,704	3,570	96.38	134	3.62
	1973	3,982	3,863	97.01	119	2.99
	1972	4,039	3,909	96.78	130	3.22
Technicians	1976	1,732	1,571	90.70	161	9.30
	1975	1,779	1,612	90.61	167	9.39
	1974	1,952	1,762	90.27	190	9.73
	1973	2,204	1,981	89.88	223	10.12
	1972	2,149	1,915	89.11	234	10.89
Sales Force	1976	1,210	1,202	99.34	8	0.66
	1975	1,489	1,482	99.53	7	0.47
	1974	1,628	1,622	99.63	6	0.37
	1973	1,641	1,637	99.76	4	0.24
	1972	1,724	1,720	99.77	4	0.23
Office Force	1976	5,910	2,090	35.36	3,820	64.64
	1975	6,046	2,238	37.02	3,808	62.98
	1974	6,675	2,621	39.27	4,054	60.73
	1973	7,491	2,993	39.95	4,498	60.05
	1972	7,857	3,135	39.90	4,722	60.10
Craft Persons	1976	5,259	5,240	99.64	19	0.36
	1975	5,502	5,494	99.85	8	0.15
	1974	5,213	5,203	99.81	10	0.19
	1973	5,466	5,453	99.76	13	0.24
	1972	5,409	5,405	99.93	4	0.23

Table 12-1
Bellco Employment Statistics

*Total number of employees in 1972 — 33,441; in 1974, — 28,151.

The following pages will help you apply the Guide.

Step 1 — Organizing and Classifying Information (Chapter 8)

The statistics in Table 12-1 reveal many things. How are you to sort it all out and come up with some ideas to solve an apparent problem?

Pore over the data. What does it reveal to you? How many ways can you find to classify it? Can you determine a purpose or contention which the particular classification could support?

For instance, suppose you disagreed with Mr. Belliston; you might present the data on women managers as follows:

> The number of women managers has more than doubled in five years (from 42 to 89), while at the same time the number of men in managerial positions has actually declined by 135 (4,288 to 4,153).

Your purpose in presenting the data this way would be to counter Mr. Belliston's contention that the company is not making an effort to get more women into managerial positions. That's a weak argument; and you would need much more support. It is included only to show that there are many ways to classify and interpret the data. See how many you can come up with before you start to plan your response. There are six categories of employment; there are actual numbers of employees; there are percentages; there are total employment figures and figures broken down into employment categories and male/female categories; the data cover five years. Work with as many categories as you can at first before you narrow it down to your key supporting points.

Step 2 — Planning (Chapter 8)

Now that you have sketched, written about, or diagrammed the statistics and have organized them into some meaningful pattern, you are ready to apply them. How are you going to do this? You need to *plan* your approach to the memo.

Paragraphs 8.17 and 8.18 tell you how to analyze the requirements of your memo. Follow the suggestions listed there. For instance, since *you* are the data analyst and the writer, *you* decide on the focal point of your memo. You could emphasize the problem, the solution, both. How will you clarify the purpose of the memo? What limitations will you impose on the document? One limitation is that you have only the one page of statistics with which to work.

Ask yourself the six questions. Decide on your answers; decide on what and where you will put emphasis. Be consistent. Write out your questions and answers so that they make sense to you.

Now you're ready to write the rough draft.

Step 3 — Writing the Rough Draft (Chapter 10)

Skip the formal outline because this is a short memo (1–2 pages) and because what you have already done in classifying, organizing, and planning constitute an outline. However, take one interim step between planning and writing the rough draft. From your planning sheet, list your purpose, focal point, and the main supporting points. Put them in a priority order. Write out possible courses of action, and put those in priority order. You are now ready to write the memo.

Apply the ideas in Chapter 10. Chapter 4 describes writing styles you can use in your memo: narrative, definition, description. You don't have to use them all. You can use one, or a combination. For instance, definition and description often go together.

Step 4 — Reviewing and Revising (Chapter 11)

You just can't do enough of this. Check your rough draft against the suggestions in Chapter 11. The first half of the chapter tells you how to check out the *sense* of what you've written. The second half tells you how to revise the expression to make it clearer and more concise.

Step 5 — Checking the Details (Chapter 12)

Read your final, typed memo. Check specifically for the problems discussed in Chapter 12, particularly those noted in paragraphs 12.2 to 12.9.

BUSINESS LETTER FORMATS ☞

APPENDIX A

T here are four basic business letter formats shown in this appendix.

1. The full-block style — Figure A-1.
2. The modified-block style — Figure A-2.
3. The semiblock style —Figure A-3.
4. The nonletterhead, personal business letter — Figure A-4.

Any one of the above styles is appropriate for a business letter. Your choice often depends on your sense of aesthetics. What do you think looks pleasing on the page? The format chosen should minimize attention to itself and maximize attention to the content of the letter.

None of the styles listed includes a subject line. If one were to be included, it would replace the salutation. While subject lines are useful in up-front letters, they can cause problems in the convincer (see Chapter 3). The subject line is usually a phrase describing briefly the subject of the letter, such as: Delay of Shipment. Sounds harmless enough, but in a convincer you want to prepare the reader by presenting the reasons for the delay before breaking the news to him.

Pasadena, Ca. 91706

June 5, 19__

Mr. James R. Link
Link Engineering Company
500 East Mountain Street
Lynn, Massachusetts

Dear Mr. Link

Figure A-1
Full-block Style.

The style of this letter is full-block. Since every line starts
at the left margin, the letter is easier for the typist to set
up, and it is neat and straightforward looking.

Open punctuation is used. Notice that there is no punctuation
after the salutation or the complimentary close. In fact, the
only commas used outside the body separate day and year in
the date line and city and state in the inside address.

Sincerely

Frank Stein
Personnel Manager

ed

Enclosure 1

Pasadena, California 91706

June 5, 19__

Mr. James R. Link
Link Engineering Company
500 East Mountain Street
Lynn, Massachusetts

Dear Mr. Link:

The modified-block style really doesn't differ much from the
full-block style shown in Figure A-1. The date line is no
longer along the left margin (it could even be centered on
the page below the letterhead). The complimentary close is
placed to the right of the center.

Punctuation in this letter is mixed. A colon is used after the
salutation; a comma is used after the complimentary close. The
choice of whether to use open or mixed punctuation is yours.

                    Sincerely,

                    Frank Stein
                    Personnel Manager

Figure A-2
*Modified-block
Style.*

Pasadena, California 91706

June 5, 19__

Mr. James R. Link
Link Engineering Company
500 East Mountain Street
Lynn, Massachusetts

Figure A–3
Semiblock Style.

Dear Mr. Link:

The semiblock style really doesn't differ much from the full-block style shown in Figure A-1. The data line is no longer along the left margin (it could even be centered on the page below the letterhead). The complimentary close is placed to the right of the center.

The semiblock style is the same as the modified-block with one exception: paragraphs are indented.

Punctuation in this letter is mixed. A colon is used after the salutation; a comma is used after the complimentary close. The choice of whether to use open or mixed punctuation is yours.

Sincerely,

Frank Stein
Personnel Manager

2770 East Spring Road
Huntsville, Alabama
June 5, 19__

Mr. James R. Link
Link Engineering Company
500 East Mountain Street
Lynn, Massachusetts

Dear Mr. Link

Since I do not have letterhead paper, I have typed my return
address at the top right-hand corner of the page. The return
address block includes the date I wrote this letter.

Sincerely,

William Lester

Figure A-4
*Nonletterhead,
Personal Business
Style.*

SAMPLE
TECHNICAL PROPOSAL ☞
APPENDIX B

This sample technical proposal was written in response to a U.S. government agency's request for proposal (RFP). It contains some unique readability features which were commended by the agency receiving the proposal. These features are:

1. *A Cross-Reference Table of Contents.* This feature allows an evaluator to select a feature of his RFP and immediately find where the corresponding response is in the Bellco proposal. Often evaluations are performed by teams of specialists. If one evaluator is interested in Command and Control, he can refer to that line in the table of contents to find that his section is discussed on page 4–44 of the Bellco proposal. This is an added convenience to him, saving him time and energy.

2. *A Combined Introduction and Capabilities Section.* Bellco felt that its competitive strength was its related experience — programs completed successfully that were relevant to the new requirements. The best place to present this experience in brief form is in the introduction. (A separate, detailed capabilities volume was also submitted.)

3. A Summary Begins Each Section. Very brief one-, two- or three-sentence summaries are set off at the beginning of each major section or module. This allows the busy executive or contract officer (who wouldn't be interested in the detail anyway) to get the essentials of the proposal by merely thumbing through the volume, reading only the first few sentences of each section. Technical evaluators, too, can benefit from this proposal design in that they can "survey" the entire proposal before settling on their particular section.

4. A Modular Approach Is Used. The proposal is designed around self-contained modules. Thus, Section 1 is complete with text and figures, Section 2 is complete with text and figures, and so on. Ideally the text and illustration are on facing pages, thus enabling the evaluator to read the text and refer to the figure simultaneously, without searching throughout the book for the representative figure or table.

These four unique proposal design features are aimed at achieving one result: making the proposal easier to read! Only Sections 1 and 2 of the proposal are provided in this sample. The remaining two sections would follow the same format.

A PROPOSAL FOR

A METEOROLOGICAL SATELLITE SENSOR SYSTEM

Proposal No. 2573

Volume I -- Technical

September 19__

A Proposal to

National Aeronautics and Space Administration

Washington, D. C.

Prepared by

Quality Environment Division

Pasadena, California 91706

FOREWORD

        This technical proposal adheres strictly to the require-
ments of the Request for Proposal with respect to sections and
their content. A "thematic modular" format has been followed
to permit the reader to view technical illustrations directly
while reading the text, thereby aiding the continuity of
thought. In addition, brief summary statements are provided at
the beginning of each module.

Proposal No. 2573

TABLE OF CONTENTS

FIGURES

TABLES

CROSS-REFERENCE TABLE OF CONTENTS

HARDWARE SEGMENT SPECIFICATION

Topic	REQUEST FOR PROPOSAL Para No.	BELLCO PROPOSAL NO. 2573 Page No.
Beamwidth	3.1.1.2	4-51
Beam Efficiency	3.1.1.3	4-51
Scan Plane Alignment	3.1.1.4	4-51
Scene Scan Station Distribution	3.1.1.5	3-1
Station Repeatability	3.1.1.6	4-54
Interface Alignment	3.1.1.7	By Design
Scan Timing	3.1.1.8	4-44
Auto Mode	3.1.1.8.1	4-44
Synchronized Mode	3.1.1.8.2	4-44
Spectral Intervals	3.1.2.1	3-1
NETD	3.1.2.2	4-49
Calibration Uncertainty	3.1.2.3	4-49
Dynamic Range	3.1.2.4	3-1
Calibration Sources	3.1.2.5	3-1
Thermal Control	3.1.2.6	4-80
Temperature Changes	3.1.2.7	4-28
Linearity	3.1.2.8	4-42
Polarization	3.1.2.9	4-10
Data Format	3.1.3	4-44
Operability	3.1.4	4-82
Prelaunch Environments	3.1.4.1	4-75
Launch Environments	3.1.4.2	4-75
Operational Environment	3.1.4.3	4-75
Reliability	3.1.4.4	4-82
Maintainability	3.1.4.5	4-82
Data	3.2.1.1	4-44
Command and Control	3.2.1.2	4-44
Power	3.2.1.3	4-65
Equipment Status Telemetry	3.2.1.4	4-44
Weight	3.2.3.1	4-70
Angular Momentum	3.2.3.2	4-54
Magnetic Dipole	3.2.3.3	By Design
Footprint and Volume	3.2.3.4	3-7
AGE Performance	3.3	4-84
Production Testing	4.1	4-74
AVE Qualification Testing	4.2	4-74
Flight AVE	4.3	4-74
AGE Testing	4.4	4-84
Mechanical/Thermal Simulator	5.0	2-1

CROSS-REFERENCE TABLE OF CONTENTS

SOFTWARE SEGMENT SPECIFICATION

Topic	REQUEST FOR PROPOSAL Para No.	BELLCO PROPOSAL NO. 2573 Page No.
Data Processing	3.1	4-0 to 4-31
Operating Environment	3.1.1	4-0, 4-18 to 4-36
Input Data	3.1.2	4-0, 4-18 to 4-29
Other Data	3.1.3	4-0, 4-18, 4-22
Data Location	3.1.4	4-0, 4-18, 4-22
Operator Interaction	3.1.5	4-0, 4-18, 4-20
Option 1	3.1.5.1	4-0, 4-20
Option 2	3.1.5.2	4-0, 4-20
Option 3	3.1.5.3	4-0, 4-20
Option 4	3.1.5.4	4-0, 4-20
Option 5	3.1.5.5	4-0, 4-20
Calibration	3.1.6	4-0, 4-18, 4-22, 4-28
Angular Dependence	3.1.7.1	4-8 to 4-12
Polarization	3.1.7.2	4-0, 4-10, 4-12, 4-30
Antenna Pattern	3.1.7.3	3-2, 4-10, 4-30
Background	3.1.7.4	3-3, 4-10, 4-12, 4-30
Precipitation	3.1.7.5	3-2, 4-0, 4-14
Inversion Algorithm	3.1.8	4-6 to 4-16
D-Matrices	3.1.8.1	3-4, 4-2 to 4-6
D-Matrix Update	3.1.8.2	3-2, 4-0, 4-30 to 4-38
Heights	3.1.9	3-2, 4-0, 4-16
Brightness File	3.1.10.1	4-0, 4-18, 4-22
Temperature Height File	3.1.10.2	4-0, 4-18, 4-24
Diagnostics	3.1.10.3	4-0, 4-18, 4-20
Timeliness	3.2.1	4-26
Storage	3.2.2	4-26
Efficiency	3.2.3	3-4, 4-0, 4-26
Maintainability	3.2.4	4-18
Program Failure	3.2.5	4-18, 4-20
Documentation	3.2.6	4-18
Product Performance Verification	4.0	4-18

Section 1 - Related Technology Programs

BELLCO TECHNICAL SKILLS AND EXPERIENCE SATISFY TOTAL REQUIREMENTS

Proven performance in the fields of spaceborne sensor instrumentation and system integrated data processing techniques summarizes the Bellco background relative to the requirements. This hardware-software experience and capability is combined within one company.

Successful delivery of a multichannel temperature sounding system requires a thorough understanding of the interrelationship of EM theory, atmospheric physics, sensor hardware, and data processing so that a well-integrated and optimized system is obtained. Bellco, with its in-depth capabilities in spaceborne sensor hardware and sensor data processing, provides the necessary disciplines and background for providing a totally integrated hardware/software system. The systems team combines these talents and capabilities to unify the sensor/atmospheric/software interfaces and to establish an efficient, optimized design.

As can be seen from the matrix in Table B-1, this capability has evolved from successful performance on many contract and company-sponsored programs. Programs described in the matrix are: Meteorological Applications Study, Weather Instruments, Electrically Scanning Sensor for Weather Satellite and Company-Sponsored Technology Program. Though Bellco has been active in the field of microwave radiometry for approximately 15 years and in the data processing field even longer, only the more recent and relevant programs are included in this tabulation. These programs have included theoretical studies, the development of spaceborne sensor systems, the implementation of operational data processing systems, and the development of key sensor components. The personnel who have provided key contributions on these programs are scheduled for similar contributions on this program.

Recognizing the refinements that were necessary in both the sensor hardware area and the software area to minimize the elements of risk to the Government, Bellco undertook several company-sponsored efforts in these areas. Specifically, an improved multiple regression method of data inversion was developed which is independent of surface backgrounds (see Section 4.2). Simulated inversions for typical zonal atmospheres have verified the power of this inversion matrix concept. Hardware efforts have reduced the shrouded atenna, broadband mixer/IF and vane modulator concepts to successfully operating developmental models.

B-9

TABLE B-1

BELLCO PROGRAMS OF RELEVANCE

Program Title and Year	Customer and Contract No.	Relevance	Key Personnel and Responsibility	Contributions
Meteorological Applications Study 1975	U.S. Govt. Agency No. 1234	This study established a feasible operational approach to profiling atmospheric temperature over land and ocean surfaces. This study also defined sensor hardware and data inversion requirements.	L. Vinci Program Manager	Conducted sensor tradeoff study and established design feasibility within prescribed payload constraints.
Weather Instruments 1970-74	U.S. Govt. Agency No. 1005	Bellco has previously provided space qualified sensor hardware for meteorological applications. This sensor has been functioning satisfactorily in space since its launch in December 1972.	J. Lee, Project Systems Engineer; W. Healy, Antenna Design; M. Jones, Project Engineer	Performed system configuration design. Designed low-loss scanning antenna system. Technical responsibility for design, fabrication assembly, integration, and test of unit.
Electrically Scanning Sensor System for Weather Satellite 1968-74	U.S. Govt. Agency No. 955	Space-qualified processing concepts similar to that proposed herein.	K. Stanley, Project Systems Engineer; R. Mire, Project Engineer; J. Bilco, Ground equipment design	Configured signal processor subsystem. Technical management program. Designed rack-mounted ground equipment.
Company-Funded Programs	Bellco			

Section 2 - Statement of the Problem

DESIGN KEYED TO GEOPHYSICAL CHARACTERISTICS

The hardware and software tradeoffs necessary to optimize the performance are the result of a comprehensive analysis involving equipment state-of-the-art, desired coverage, and profiling accuracy. These are influenced by both the earth's surface features and the electromagnetic characteristics of the atmosphere.

The characteristics of the atmosphere are determined primarily by the absorption and emission characteristics of oxygen. Since the mixing ratio of oxygen is constant in the atmosphere, the contribution of a particular layer of the atmosphere to the total radiation detected by a spaceborne sensor is controlled by the air temperature. A physical basis for deducing the air temperature profile by an analysis of sensor signals has been established. This analysis will be performed by an algorithm which will be discussed in detail in succeeding pages of this volume.

Since the underlying earth surface also contributes to the detected radiation at those frequencies responding to the lowest portion of the atmosphere, the software must be designed to eliminate the effects of the surface. A unique, highly efficient algorithm has been developed.

Solution of the overall problem will be accomplished in accordance with the details discussed in this proposal which is configured to address the basic tasks described in the RFP. A summary of these tasks is presented here to assist in the understanding of Bellco's approach to the solution of the problem.

Earth-viewing and calibration-scanning geometry are shown in Figure B-1. Notice that two calibration positions are provided, cold sky and hot.

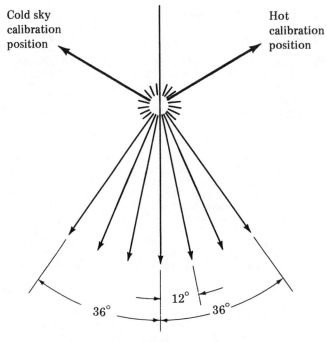

Figure B-1. Earth-Viewing and Calibration-Scanning Geometry.

TECHNICAL REPORT ☞
APPENDIX C

While only those reports submitted to an agency of the Department of Defense must adhere to MIL-STD-847A, we include that standard here (somewhat abridged) as Appendix C because it does describe in detail an effective and orderly format. In addition, the document follows its own formula and is, therefore, itself a good example.

The Table of Contents is also a very fine outline. For instance, Paragraph 1 concerns the scope (coverage) of the report. Under Scope, the authors include — Purpose, 1.1, and Application, 1.2. As a part of Application, the authors include — Forms of Reports, 1.2.1, which also includes Manuscript Copy, 1.2.1.1, Reproducible Copy, 1.2.1.2, and so on.

This abridged document and Chapter 10 of the text should provide enough guidelines to help you prepare any formal scientific or technical report — whether it be in engineering, medicine, or any other scientific field.

MIL-STD-847A
31 January 1973
SUPERSEDING
MIL-STD-847 (USAF)
25 February 1965

MILITARY STANDARD

FORMAT REQUIREMENTS FOR SCIENTIFIC AND TECHNICAL REPORTS

PREPARED BY OR FOR THE DEPARTMENT OF DEFENSE

FSC - MISC
MISC-0763

MIL-STD-847A
31 January 1973

CONTENTS

MIL-STD-847A
31 January 1973

CONTENTS

MIL-STD-847A
31 January 1973

FIGURES

MIL-STD-847A
31 January 1973

FORMAT REQUIREMENTS FOR SCIENTIFIC AND TECHNICAL REPORTS

PREPARED BY OR FOR THE DEPARTMENT OF DEFENSE

1. SCOPE

1.1 <u>Purpose</u>. This standard establishes format requirements for scientific and technical reports prepared by or for the departments and agencies of the Department of Defense. Its purposes are to aid the interchange of scientific and technical information and to reduce the costs of preparing, storing, retrieving, reproducing, and distributing such reports.

1.2 <u>Application</u>.

1.2.1 Forms of reports. This standard applies to scientific and technical reports (for definition see paragraph 3.1, Technical report) under the DoD scientific and technical information program in any of the following forms:

1.2.1.1 Manuscript copy: Text and illustrations suitably assembled for review and editing.

1.2.1.2 Reproducible copy: A set of text and illustration pages that has been corrected, laid out, and made ready for reproduction.

1.2.1.3 Reproduced copy: Reports that have been duplicated or printed and are ready for distribution.

1.2.1.4 Microform: Reports photographed in miniature on film.

1.2.2 Excluded documents.

1.2.2.1 Letter reports, manuals, catalogs, and computer printouts. This standard does not apply to letter reports, training manuals, catalogs, administrative or fiscal reports, or reports consisting only of computer printouts.

1.2.2.2 Intelligence reports. Assignment of responsibility for format for technical intelligence reports prepared by or for the Defense Intelligence Agency is contained in DIA Manual 75-1, "Scientific and Technical Intelligence Production," and is excluded from the scope of this standard.

MIL-STD-847A
31 January 1973

1.2.2.3 Preprints, reprints, books, theses, and dissertations.
Journal article preprints, reprints, commercially published books or
chapters of books, theses, or dissertations submitted in lieu of a
technical report are excluded from compliance with the provisions of
this standard except that the Report Documentation Page, DD Form 1473,
shall be made a part of each copy of such publication which is submitted to the Department of Defense.

1.2.2.4 Waiver of requirements. The Commanding Officer, Technical
Director or equivalent, of the organization responsible for the conduct
of the work set forth in the report, for example, Naval Weapons Laboratory,
may grant a waiver of the requirements contained herein except for the
inclusion of a DD Form 1473 (see paragraph 5.3.1, Report Documentation
Page, DD Form 1473) and other mandatory requirements, for example,
security markings. Such waivers will be granted on a case by case basis.

2.   REFERENCED DOCUMENTS

The issues of the following documents in effect on the date of invitation for bids form a part of this standard to the extent specified
herein.

(a) DoD 5200.1-R, "Information Security Program Regulation."
     (Available from the Naval Publications and Forms Center,
     5801 Tabor Avenue, Philadelphia, Pennsylvania, 19120, and
     the Superintendent of Documents, U.S. Government Printing
     Office, Washington, D.C., 20402.)
(b) DoD Directive 5200.20, "Distribution Statements on Technical
     Documents." (Available from the Naval Publications and Forms
     Center, 5801 Tabor Avenue, Philadelphia, Pennsylvania, 19120.)
(c) DoD 5220.22-M, "Industrial Security Manual for Safeguarding
     Classified Information." (Available to Navy activities from:
     Naval Publications and Forms Center, 5801 Tabor Avenue,
     Philadelphia, Pennsylvania, 19120; to Army and Air Force
     activities from: Commanding Officer, U.S. Army AG Publica-
     tions Center, 2800 Eastern Boulevard, Baltimore, Maryland,
     21220; to others from: Superintendent of Documents, U.S.
     Government Printing Office, Washington, D.C., 20402.)
(d) "Armed Services Procurement Regulation." (Available from the
     Naval Publications and Forms Center, 5801 Tabor Avenue,
     Philadelphia, Pennsylvania, 19120)
(e) "Government Printing and Binding Regulations." (Available from
     the Joint Committee on Printing, U.S. Congress, Committee
     Room S-151, U.S. Capitol, Washington, D.C., 20510.)
(f) "Government Paper Specification Standards." (Available from
     the Joint Committee on Printing, U.S. Congress, Committee
     Room S-151, U.S. Capitol, Washington, D.C., 20510.)

MIL-STD-847A
31 January 1973

(g) "Abstracting Scientific and Technical Reports of Defense-
Sponsored RDT&E." Defense Documentation Center, AD-667 000.
(Available from the National Technical Information Service,
Springfield, Virginia, 22151.)

3. DEFINITIONS

3.1 <u>Technical report</u>. Any preliminary or final technical document
written for the permanent record to document results obtained from, or
recommendations made on, Department of Defense sponsored or cosponsored
scientific and technical activities.

3.2 <u>Controlling DoD office</u>. The DoD activity, under whose immediate
program a document is generated, whether the work was done in-house or
by contract. In the case of joint sponsorship, the controlling office
is determined by advance agreement, and may be either party, or a group
or committee representing more than one activity or service or agency.

4. GENERAL REQUIREMENTS (Not applicable)

5. DETAILED FORMAT REQUIREMENTS

5.1 <u>Order of elements</u>. Although all reports do not necessarily
contain all the following elements, those that are used will appear in
the following order with the abstract appearing only on the Report
Documentation Page, DD Form 1473:

5.1.1 Front matter. Front cover (required)
Report Documentation Page, DD Form 1473 (required)
Summary
Preface
Table of contents
List of illustrations
List of tables

5.1.2 Body of report. Introduction
Main text
Conclusions
Recommendations

5.1.3 Reference material. References
Bibliography
Appendixes
Glossary of terms
List of abbreviations, acronyms, and symbols
Index
Distribution list
Back cover (required)

3

MIL-STD-847A
31 January 1973

5.2 Front cover.

5.2.1 Outside front cover. Self covers (of the same paper as the text) or separate covers of different paper from the text are acceptable. Include on the cover the information shown in the following paragraphs plus special markings, such as security classification and schedule for downgrading and declassification. Military Services regulations for marking classified information shall be followed. (See DoD 5200.1-R, DoD 5220.22-M, and the respective Service implementing regulations.) Group related items as shown in Figure 1.

5.2.1.1 Group I. Report number. Each report will carry a unique alphanumeric designation, or report number, in the upper portion of the cover using one of the following types:

(a) An alphanumeric designation provided by the controlling office (for example, FML-RD-68-100); or, if none has been assigned,

(b) An alphanumeric designation established by the performing organization (for example, ORNL-8737); or if none has been established,

(c) An alphanumeric designation derived from the contract or grant number (for example, AF19618-69-C-0001).

5.2.1.2 Group II

(a) Title and subtitle. Display the title prominently and make it indicate clearly and briefly the subject of the report. Set subtitle, if used, in smaller type or otherwise subordinate it to the main title. When a report is prepared in more than one volume, repeat the primary title and have the subtitles identify specific volumes.

(b) Author(s). Give the name(s) of the author(s) in conventional order (for example, John R. Doe, or if author prefers, J. Robert Doe). An exception to the "Government Printing and Binding Regulations," granted by JCP, permits authors' names to appear on the covers of scientific and technical reports.

(c) Performing organization name and address. For contractor reports, give name, city, state, and ZIP Code. List no more than two levels of an organizational hierarchy.

(d) Date. Each report will carry a date consisting of at least the month and year.

(e) Type of report and period covered. Indicate interim, final, etc., and, if applicable, dates covered.

MIL-STD-847A
31 January 1973

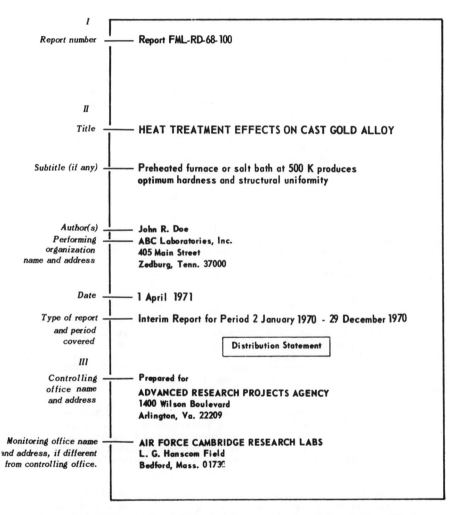

I
Report number ———— **Report FML-RD-68-100**

II
Title ———— **HEAT TREATMENT EFFECTS ON CAST GOLD ALLOY**

Subtitle (if any) ———— **Preheated furnace or salt bath at 500 K produces
optimum hardness and structural uniformity**

Author(s) ———— **John R. Doe**
Performing ———— **ABC Laboratories, Inc.**
organization **405 Main Street**
name and address **Zedburg, Tenn. 37000**

Date ———— **1 April 1971**

Type of report ———— **Interim Report for Period 2 January 1970 - 29 December 1970**
and period
covered

Distribution Statement

III
Controlling ———— **Prepared for**
office name **ADVANCED RESEARCH PROJECTS AGENCY**
and address **1400 Wilson Boulevard**
Arlington, Va. 22209

Monitoring office name ———— **AIR FORCE CAMBRIDGE RESEARCH LABS**
and address, if different **L. G. Hanscom Field**
from controlling office. **Bedford, Mass. 01730**

Figure 1. Sample unclassified report cover (reduced in size). Other
layouts and type faces may be used if related items are grouped in the
manner indicated. Required security markings must be added to covers
of classified reports.

MIL-STD-847A
31 January 1973

(f) Distribution statement. (See DoD Directive 5200.20.)
The same statement that appears here must also appear
in Block 16 of the Report Documentation Page, DD Form
1473.

5.2.1.3 Group III

(a) Controlling office. (Equates to sponsoring/funding
activity. For definition see paragraph 3.2, Controlling
DoD office.) The name and mailing address, including
ZIP Code, will appear in the lower portion of the front
cover. The words "Prepared for" will be placed immediately
above the sponsoring activity's name on all contractor/
grantee reports.
(b) Monitoring agency. The name and mailing address, including
ZIP Code, will appear under the controlling office in
those cases where the administrative responsibility for a
project, contract, or grant has been delegated to another
activity.

5.2.2 Inside front cover. A review and approval statement and
special notices such as reproduction limitations, espionage, legal and
supersedure information, safety precautions, sponsor's disclaimers, compliance with special regulations, or disposition instructions will be
included here or on the outside front cover.

5.3 Introductory material.

5.3.1 Report Documentation Page, DD Form 1473. (See Figure 6.)
Include a completed DD Form 1473 (Revised), Report Documentation Page,
as the first right-hand page after the cover in each report. (See
Armed Services Procurement Regulation, paragraph 4-113.) This page is
intended to replace the title page and revises the DD Form 1473 formerly
required at the end of each technical report. Instructions for its
completion are given in the appendix.

5.3.2 Summary. A summary may be included to provide a digest of
the report, to explain the reason for the initiation of the work, and
to outline principal conclusions and recommendations. A summary may
be used to give more information on the content of the report than can
be presented in the abstract entered on the Report Documentation Page,
DD Form 1473.

5.3.3 Preface. If a preface is used, it may show the relation of
the work reported on to associated efforts, give credit for the use of
copyrighted material, or acknowledge significant assistance received.

MIL-STD-847A
31 January 1973

5.3.4 Table of contents. Seldom used in a report of eight pages or less. If used, list principal headings as they appear in the report with the page numbers on which the headings occur. Start the table of contents on a new right-hand page.

5.3.5 List of illustrations. Include only if considered essential. List figure number, legend, and page number for each illustration. Abbreviate lengthy legends.

5.3.6 List of tables. Include only if considered essential. List table number, heading, and page number for each table. Abbreviate lengthy headings.

5.4 <u>Body of report</u>.

5.4.1 General. Start the first section on a new page. This section usually provides background information and work objectives. Succeeding sections may describe work procedures, apparatus involved, tests performed, results achieved, and related matters, as appropriate. The terminal sections usually present conclusions and recommendations.

5.4.2 Headings. Headings will stand out from the text with their relative importance apparent. They may be prepared on a standard typewriter or on composing equipment. Typical heading styles are illustrated in Figure 2.

METHODS ————— *First-order head*

Third-order head   Macroplankton ————— *Second-order head*

Sampling—The larger and more sparse macroplankton were sampled . . . . .
. . . .

METHODS ————— *First-order head*

Macroplankton ————— *Second-order head*

SAMPLING ————— *Third-order head*

The larger and more sparse macroplankton were sampled . . . .
. . . .

Figure 2. Two examples of headings. Top example shows standard typewriter headings; bottom example shows headings prepared on composing equipment. Other type styles may be used as long as the headings stand out and relative importance is apparent.

MIL-STD-847A
31 January 1973

5.4.3 **Numbering systems.** Number headings and paragraphs only when needed for clarity.

5.5 Reference material.

5.5.1 **References a d bibliography.** Include complete identification of references on bottom of pag, where first cited to aid in reading from microform. When references are numerous, they should be repeated in a reference list in the back of the report. Arrange bibliographic entries not included in the text but supplied as supplementary information under "Bibliography." Present entries in a uniform style. Include authors, titles, sources, identifying numbers, publication dates, and applicable security classifications.

5.5.2 **Appendixes.** When one or more appendixes are used, designate them Appendix A, Appendix B, etc. Number figures, tables, and equations with the letter designation of the appendix in which they fall. Each appendix will be titled. Start the first appendix on a new page.

5.5.3 **Glossary of terms.** Define unusual terms either in the text or as a footnote the first time they are used in the text. When many such terms are used, list them in alphabetical order with definitions in a glossary.

5.5.4 **Abbreviations, acronyms, and symbols.** Define abbreviations, acronyms, and symbols when first introduced in the text. If they are numerous, include a list of definitions in the reference material.

5.5.5 **Index.** If an index is included, make it as complete as the nature of the report and its probable usage requires.

5.5.6 **Distribution list.** A distribution list may be included within a report. If included, it will appear at the end of the report.

5.6 Illustrations.

5.6.1 **General.** Treat illustrations consistently throughout a report. Prepare them so that details and callouts (labels) will be clearly legible after final reduction. When practical, crop or mask photographs to eliminate insignificant detail. Do not add a border frame or use background tones in line drawings unless they contribute substantially to clarity. For reproducible copy, submit only clean tone or line art and only original photographs rather than screened (halftone) reproductions when practical.

8

MIL-STD-847A
31 January 1973

5.6.2 Placement. Locate illustrations as near as possible after
the first text reference except in special situations, such as a report
containing only a few text pages and many illustrations. In such cases,
place the illustrations in numerical sequence in the back of the report.
Unless it is not possible to do so and maintain readability, place illustrations so that they may be viewed without turning the page sideways.
If this is not possible, place the illustrations sideways so that they
can be seen by rotating the page clockwise.

5.6.3 Callouts (Labels). So far as practical, place callouts
horizontally, unboxed, and near the item called out as shown in Figure 3.
Make callouts consistent in size and typeface throughout a report. Use
lettering of at least 8-point or 1/9-inch high in a final reproduced
size.

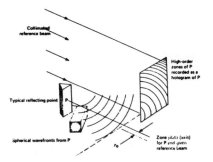

Figure 3. Placement of callouts in illustrations.

5.6.4 Color. Color will not be used unless specifically authorized
by the controlling office as the only means of presenting data clearly.
Often screens, crosshatching, reverses, dots, or similar techniques can
be effective substitutes for color (Figure 4).

5.6.5 Foldouts. Wherever possible, avoid the use of oversize illustrations that must be folded. Often a large illustration can be
divided to appear on facing pages. When foldouts cannot be avoided make
them begin on a right-hand page and number as one page.

5.6.6 Numbering. Number illustrations to which reference is made
in the text in Arabic numerals, preceded by the word "Figure." Number
illustrations within appendixes in a manner consistent with the appendix
designation.

9

MIL-STD-847A
31 January 1973

5.6.7 Legends. Accompany each illustration, except self-explanatory
sketches, by a descriptive legend. Place the legend under the illustration following the figure number.

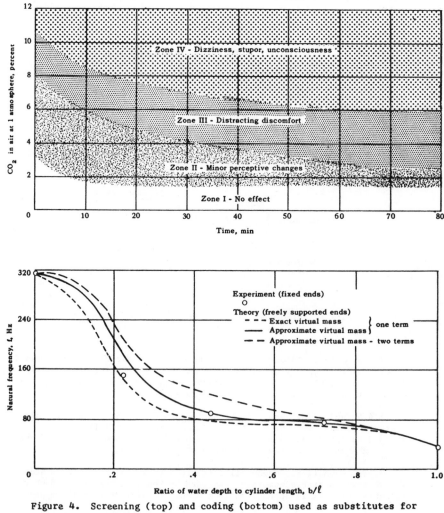

Figure 4. Screening (top) and coding (bottom) used as substitutes for
color.

MIL-STD-847A
31 January 1973

5.7 <u>Tables</u>.

5.7.1 General. Tables should be as simple as possible so that the reader can easily grasp the meaning of the data. Avoid vertical and horizontal lines wherever spacing can be used effectively. Use letters and numbers in tables that will be at least 8-point or 1/9-inch high in the final reproduced report. Letters and numbers on printout sheets from electronically tabulated data used for direct reproduction should be sharp and unbroken. See Figure 5.

TABLE 1. SHORT-TIME XXXXXXXXXXXXXXXXXXXXX ◄———*Heading*

Boxhead

Temperature (K)	Specimen type[a]	Ultimate tensile strength, (N/m^2)	Elongation between buttonheads, (cm)	Reduction of area, (percent)
Footnote reference ┘		Tungsten		
1700	1	2200×10^3	1.57	95
1900	1	1312	1.60	75
2060	1	987	.69	36
2260	1	674	.51	25
		Molybdenum		
1650	2	9301×10^3	0.95	96
1922	2	4068	1.55	99
2255	2	1472	1.75	99

[a]Recrystallized at 2370 K for 1/2 hour in vacuum.◄———*Footnote*

Figure 5. Typical table layout.

5.7.2 Placement. Locate tables as near as possible after their first text reference except in special situations, such as when a report contains only a few text pages and many tables. In such cases place the tables in numerical sequence in the back of the report. Unless it is not possible to do so and maintain readability, place tables so that they may be viewed without turning the page sideways. If this is not possible, place each table sideways so that it can be seen by rotating the page clockwise.

MIL-STD-847A
31 January 1973

5.7.3 Columns and column headings. Give applicable units of measure or degree in the column headings of tables. Do not repeat in the columns. When tables continue on two or more pages, note the continuation and repeat the column headings and rules on each page, except column headings need not be repeated on the second page for continuations on two facing pages turned sideways.

5.7.4 Numbering. Number tables in the text consecutively in Arabic numerals, preceded by the word "Table." Tables within appendixes should be numbered in a manner consistent with the appendix.

5.7.5 Headings. Give each table, except short ones run in with the text, a descriptive heading following the table number. Place heading above the table.

5.8 <u>Equations.</u>

5.8.1 General. Prepare mathematical matter with extreme care. Use machine or transfer-type composition when available. When necessary, identify symbols after first use in order to simplify reading from any type of microform, otherwise include in a separate list. Make opening and closing parentheses, brackets, and braces the same height as the tallest expression they enclose. Separate the numerator from the denominator with a line as long as the longer of the two. Center both numerator and denominator on the line.

5.8.2 Placement. Indent or center a displayed equation in the line immediately following the first text reference made to it. Break equations before an equal, plus, or multiplication sign. Align a group of separate but related equations by the equal signs and indent or center the group as a whole. Short equations not part of a series or identified by number will be placed in the text rather than displayed.

5.8.3 Numbering. Number equations which are part of a series or which are referred to in the text consecutively in Arabic numerals. Enclose each number in parentheses at the right margin on the last line of the equation to which it refers. Equations within appendixes should be numbered in a manner consistent with the appendix.

5.9 <u>Production.</u>

5.9.1 Composition.

5.9.1.1 Type size. The size of type for the main text shall provide for final page copy, including reproduction thereof, in which letters and numbers are at least as large as 8-point type; 10-point, or equivalent, is preferred.

5.9.1.2 Line spacing. Use single or 1½ spacing for reports prepared by typewriter for reproduction, except when double spacing between
lines is necessary to assure clarity of equations or symbols. Use 1½ or
double spacing for manuscripts.

5.9.1.3 Margins. Use margins of at least 1 inch on all sides of
text pages.

5.9.1.4 Columns. Prepare text pages with a single column, not
necessarily justified on the right margin, unless the controlling agency
authorizes justification or use of more than one column.

5.9.1.5 Page numbering and usage. All pages following the Report
Documentation Page, DD Form 1473, will be numbered consecutively at the
bottom center in Arabic numerals. Separate volumes may be numbered independently. Odd-numbered pages are right-hand pages and even-numbered
pages are left-hand pages. Use both sides of the sheet to the maximum
extent practical.

5.9.1.6 Typewriter ribbons. Use black ribbon to type reproducible
copy. Carbon ribbon is preferred.

5.9.2 Duplication vs. printing. Contractors or grantees shall not
become prime sources of printing for departments or agencies unless so
authorized by the Joint Committee on Printing nor shall printing be a
preplanned contractual requirement. Duplicating shall conform to the
requirements of the "Government Printing and Binding Regulations."

5.9.3 Workmanship. Filled-in or broken letters, illegible text or
illustrations (including lettering) or similar imperfections are not
acceptable. Only reproduced reports that will be legible in microform
are acceptable.

5.9.4 Cover size, stock, and ink. Reproduced reports may have self
covers cut to page size or separate covers. If separate covers are used,
GPO standard 100-pound basis weight antique or vellum finish (or comparable quality) is preferred. (See "Government Paper Specification
Standards.") Black ink will be used on covers. Do not use covers with
windows.

5.9.5 Page size, stock, and ink. Reproduced reports shall be
8 X 10½ or 8½ X 11 inches in size. Use black ink on GPO standard 32- to
40-pound (or comparable quality) writing paper stock for text pages.
(See "Government Paper Specification Standards.")

25 245

MIL-STD-847A
31 January 1973

5.9.6 Binding. Bind reports by using saddle stitching or side
stitching. Other types of binding such as glued-on covers, perfect
binding, or case binding must have prior approval of the controlling
DoD office.

5.9.7 Decorative features and advertising. Only simple organizational symbols or logos are permissible. Advertising display shall
not be used.

Custodians: Preparing activity:
  Army - MU   Defense Supply Agency - DD
  Navy - NM
  Air Force - 10

Review activities:
  Army - EL, MI, ME, AV, WC,
      MR, GL, AD
  Navy - None
  Air Force - 11, 13, 17, 19
  Defense Communications Agency - DC
  Defense Nuclear Agency - DS
  National Security Agency - NS

User activities:
  Army - AT
  Navy - None
  Air Force - 18